HOW TO SEE
IN THE
SPIRIT WORLD

Mel Bond

D1319866

ISBN 978-1-882318-06-4

HOW TO SEE IN THE SPIRIT WORLD

Contents

DEDICATION

I dedicate this book to my best friend, the Lord Jesus Christ. His loving-kindness to me is better than life itself! (Psalm 63:3)

PREFACE

The purpose of this book is to teach God's people how to flow in the Supernatural of God, to glorify God, to bring masses into the kingdom of God and to bless people.

I will teach you from the Holy Scriptures, in simplicity, how to actually see in the Spirit world. You will learn how to see demon spirits for the purpose of getting rid of the root of all problems.

You will learn how to fix problems that demons have caused.

In this book, you will learn that our faith goes hand in hand with learning to see in the Spirit world.

You will learn that it is God's perfect will for people that are born again and Spirit-filled to see in the Spirit world (which is the Gift of Discerning of Spirits, I Corinthians 12:10).

A major factor for flowing with the Gift of Discerning of Spirits is being child-like in our faith, belief, trust and confidence in God's Word. Matthew 18:3: "Verily I say unto you, except ye be converted and become as little children, ye shall not enter into the kingdom of heaven."

You will learn that this is an extremely strong doctrine of God, that people in the Old Testament used often. With this in mind, know that we are of the New Testament, established upon better promises, so whatever God did for any one of the Old Testament, He will do for us today and more.

The prerequisites of being able to see in the Spirit world, which is the Gift of Discerning of Spirits, and to allow all of the Gifts of the Holy Spirit to operate in your life are: No.1. A person must be born again by accepting Jesus Christ as their Lord and Savior (John 3:3: "...except a person be born again they cannot "see" the kingdom of God," Romans 10:9,10). No. 2. A person should be filled with the Holy Spirit with the evidence of speaking in tongues (Acts 2:4). Also in John 7:39 Jesus said, "But this spake He of the Spirit, which they that believe on Him SHOULD receive: for the Holy Ghost was not yet given; because that Jesus was not yet glorified."

I am not saying if a person is not Spirit-filled they cannot operate with the Gifts of the Holy Spirit; because they did in the Old Testament. However, it was not very often, sometimes it would only happen through a prophet of God and many times only one time in their life. Today, we have a New Covenant established upon better promises and all can now receive all of the Gifts and operate with them as often as they perceive the need (John 14:12-14; Philippians 2:5).

Oceans of Eternal Unconditional Love in Jesus Christ,
Mel Bond

1

God's purpose for the Gift

I want to share with you God's purpose for humanity to allow the Gift of Discerning of Spirits to operate in their lives.

That God Would Be Glorified

In John 14:12-14 Jesus said, "...He (or she) that believeth on Me *the works*, that I do shall he (or she) do also; and greater *works* than these shall he (or she) do; because I go unto my Father."

Verse 13: "And whatsoever ye shall ask in My name, that will I do *that the Father may be glorified in the Son.*" (Note: The italicized words, "the works & works" in this passage is the Greek word, "ergon". And the fuller meaning of this Greek word is: *occupation, acts, doing, labor).*

This same Greek word, "ergon" is used 161 times in the New Testament and is used several times in reference to Jesus doing miracles. A good example is in Matthew 11:2-5: Here the works of Jesus is referred to as: blind receiving their sight, lame walking, the lepers being cleansed, the deaf

1

hearing, and the dead being raised.

The Bible clearly teaches that Jesus would cast demons out first, then He would heal the sick. Here is just a few passages showing this. If you'll read the Gospels, you'll see this pattern.

Look at Matthew 8:16: "...they brought unto Him many that were possessed with devils: and *He cast out the spirits with His Word, and healed all that were sick."*

Acts 10:38: "How God anointed Jesus of Nazareth with the Holy Ghost and with power: who went about doing good, and healing all that were oppressed of the devil; for God was with him."

In Matthew 9:6-8, Jesus healed the sick and *the multitude saw it and marveled and glorified God.*

Matthew 15:31: "...the multitude wondered, when they saw the dumb to speak, the maimed to be whole, the lame to walk, and the blind to see: and *they glorified the God of Israel."*

In Luke 13:12,13, Jesus spoke to the demon spirit and said, *"thou art loosed"* of thy infirmity and then laid His hands on her and she was healed. (Note: The italicized phrase, "thou art loosed" is the Greek word, "apoluo". This Greek word is also translated as: depart, divorce). Clearly, Jesus commanded the demon to leave first and then healed the lady.

When we look into the Spirit world and see the demon, (which is the root of the problem) and cast it out, then heal the person; God is Glorified!

People Are Blessed

When people are delivered from pain or any problem;

2

knowing it was God that did it, they are blessed. More times than I could possibly remember; seeing people living for as long as 40 years with incurable pain and then set free by the power of God's Unconditional Love, I've watched tears run down their faces. Tears of blessings, tears of great thankfulness.

Psalm 144:15 the Bible says, "Happy is that people, that is in such a case: yea, happy is that people, whose God is the Lord."

When demons are seen and cast out of people, they have no doubt that God did this and they become very happy. It's like having a problem that there is no hope of solving, and then it is totally gone; this causes people to be happy and blessed. They know it was the supernatural love and compassion of God; and they become very happy.

When God's power is present, people are delivered freely.

The Gift Opens the Door for the Supernatural

Demons are seen, where a person has a problem. And that person knows only God could reveal such a truth; it causes them to open their spirit and mind up to the realm of the Supernatural of God. It does the same for a setting where there is a group of people watching the operation of the Gift of Discerning of Spirits.

The Apostle Paul said in I Corinthians 2:4: "And my speech and my preaching was not with enticing words of man's wisdom, but in *demonstration of the Spirit and of power: V. 5. That your faith should not stand in the wisdom of men, but in the power of God.*"

The demonstration of the Holy Spirit is the Gifts of the

Holy Spirit in operation. (Notice I Corinthians 12:7-11: The manifestation of the Spirit is the Gifts of the Holy Spirit).

The demonstration of the Gifts of the Holy Spirit is really the full Gospel. Just as the Apostle Paul said that he would first preach the Word and then he would demonstrate the power of God by operating with the Gifts of the Holy Spirit or the Offices of the Holy Spirit.

The Apostle Paul did this for the purpose of people's faith standing not in just words, but in a demonstration of God. Paul said it again using different words in Romans 15:18-19; he said he was obedient with the Word, and had Signs and Wonders. He then concluded that he had FULLY PREACHED THE GOSPEL.

In Mark 16:20, Jesus said God would confirm His Word, "with Signs following". Preaching and teaching the full Gospel is allowing the Holy Spirit to confirm the Word with Signs following; with the demonstration of the Gifts of the Holy Ghost.

Once a demon spirit is seen and cast out, the person's faith has now supernaturally risen. This also sets an atmosphere where the people that are present, now have their faith increased supernaturally. In this kind of atmosphere, you now can open yourself up for more of the Gifts of the Holy Spirit. The demon that caused the problem is gone. You just cast the root of the problem out. Now, you can release the Gifts of Healings or Working of Miracles. The demon caused the problem; the demon is gone, and now God's supernatural power can fix the problem. Sort of like a mosquito; he comes and bites. You get rid of the mosquito, but now, the bite needs to be healed.

Now, since the atmosphere or the person is full of belief, you can open yourself up for other Gifts of the Holy Spirit. People are now ready to receive. My book, "Releas-

4

ing God's Anointing" will help you to release God's power for healing and miracles.

The Gift of Discerning of Spirits sets a supernatural atmosphere for all of the Gifts of the Holy Spirit. Jesus gives us some clear teaching along these lines in Mark, Chapter 6. Jesus went to Nazareth and made these statements in verse 5: "And He could there do no mighty works, save that he laid His hands upon a few sick folk, and healed them. V. 6. And He marveled, because of their unbelief."

Just the opposite takes place when there is an atmosphere of belief. The Gift of Discerning of Spirits will set an atmosphere where the other Supernatural Offices and Gifts can operate. This gives God great honor and glory and blesses people.

2

THE OFFICE VERSUS THE GIFT

Intro: All of the Gifts of the Holy Spirit have an Office that is very similar to each Gift. If we look at I Corinthians 12:8-10, clearly we read about the 9 Gifts of the Holy Spirit. As you study the Bible, you can clearly see Offices that have very similar manifestations. This is where many people get cheated out of allowing all of the Gifts of the Holy Spirit to flow through them. As it is clear, a person cannot have all of the Offices of the Holy Spirit. Offices are ordained of God, they are callings of God, they are operations that God inspires and God initiates. The Gifts belong to all of humanity, and they can all be obtained by the born again, Spirit-filled (those that speak in tongues) believer.

Let me share briefly some Scripture settings that teach about the Gifts and Offices, so we can know the difference.

Gifts of Healings Versus the Office of Healings

Let's first look at the doctrine of the Gifts of Healing.

Plainly, there are several passages in the Bible that clearly teach all born again Christians are suppose to pray for the sick that they would be healed. Look at a couple of verses that clearly validates this truth. Matthew 10:8: Jesus told us to, "Heal the sick". In Mark 16:17 it says: "And these signs shall follow them that believe; In my name... V.18: ...they shall lay hands on the sick, and they shall recover." Read John 14:12-14: "Verily, verily, I say *unto you, He that believeth* on me, the works that I do *shall he do* also; and greater works than these shall he do...." (Note: The first italicized phrase is the single Greek word, "pisteuo". This Greek word is also rendered as: a person, a believer. The word, "man" is not in this Greek word at all; the word, "he" could be in reference here, but co-equally, "she" could be used also. So accurately the word, "person" is the most valid translation. Also notice the second italicized phrase is the single Greek word, "poieo". This Greek word does not have the word, "he" within it at all, neither are there any words within this Greek word that could possibly be in reference to the word, "he". In other words, within the meaning of this word are: *appoint, bring forth, cause, execute, exercise, ordain, perform, provide, shew, shoot out, yield.* I fully understand that this phrase is directly in reference to the first italicized phrase; so accurately this second phrase would be translated: "shall people do.")

The Office of Healings

By looking at these verses, you can see that God has ordained certain people to have the Office of Healings. Someone in the Office of Healings would have more healings. Healings would be magnified, manifested more in their lives. It's sort of like all people may have a dollar but that does not make them all millionaires. A person with one dollar has only one of what a millionaire has a million of.

In I Corinthians 12:28, God talks about Offices. Look at verse 28: "And God hath set some in the Church, first apostles, secondarily prophets, thirdly teachers, after that miracles, then gifts of healings....." (Note: In this book, go to Chapter 3 and look for the subtitle: Old Strong Tradition). In this subtitle, you will plainly see in this same chapter (I Corinthians 12:7-11) that ALL of the Gifts of the Holy Spirit are for everyone (that is born again and filled with the Holy Spirit with the evidence of speaking in tongues). So right in this same chapter you can plainly see that all of Gifts are for all, and then clearly the Offices are not for all.

In verses 28-31, it is plain God is talking about Offices and not Gifts. Clearly, not all are prophets, not all are apostles, etc. Clearly, this passage is talking about Offices, and not all have all the Offices. But if you have the desire for that Office, then do as God directs in verse 31: "..covet" (the Greek word for covet is, "zeloo" and is translated as: desire, be jealous over) earnestly the best *gifts* (The italicized word, "gifts" is the Greek word,"charisma". This word is also translated as a divine gratuity, spiritual endowment, miraculous faculty, or free gift). The word, "gift" in this passage is clearly in reference to the verses prior to it. It is the closing statement of the teaching of, "Offices". Accurately, by context and by the fuller meaning of this Greek word, "charisma", gifts should be translated as, "Office"; as an Office is a Divine Spiritual endowment. I clearly understand this same word "charisma" is used in verse 9, in reference to Gifts of Healings, which are given to everyone. Notice the word, "Charisma" can be accurately translated as, "free gift". We have words in all languages that are interchangable words. For example in the English language the word, "person" can accurately be used for a woman or a man. But by the context of the sentence, it is clearly understood if it is a woman person or a man person that we are talking about.

A good understanding of knowing if you are supposed to be in the Office of Healings is checking the desires of your heart. If you have a desire in your heart to be used of God at all times for people to be healed, then it is evident that you are called in that Office. Psalm 37:4, teaches us that God gives us the desires of our heart. If it is a desire of your heart it will never go away. Romans 11:29, clearly teaches us that the gifts and callings of God are without repentance. If God put the desire in your heart to see people healed all of the time; God will not change His mind. That desire will never leave.

Gift of Tongues Versus the Office of Tongues

In this subtitle, you will be able to see that the Gift of Tongues is for everyone but the Office of Tongues is something that God initiates.

In Acts 2:4, the people that were in the upper room (notice Peter was there); they were ALL filled with the Holy Ghost, and began to speak with tongues. Then in the same chapter, after this experience that Peter had, he says in verse 38: "...Repent, and be baptized EVERY ONE OF YOU... and ye shall receive the gift of the Holy Ghost. V.39. For the promise is unto you, and to your children and to ALL ...."

Look at I Corinthians 14:5, God clearly says, "I would that ye ALL spake with tongues..." V.39: "...forbid not to speak with tongues."

Jesus taught us plainly that All SHOULD receive the gift of speaking in tongues. Read John 7:37: "...Jesus stood and cried, saying, If any man thirst, let him come unto me, and drink. V.38. He that believeth on me, as the Scripture hath said, out of his belly shall flow rivers of living water. V.39. But this spake he of the Spirit, which they that believe on him 'SHOULD RECEIVE': for the Holy Ghost was not yet given; because that Jesus was not yet glorified." (Note: Jesus was talking plainly about Acts 2:4, in which they that believed were filled with the Holy Ghost and spake in tongues).

The Office of Tongues

Again, keep in mind I Corinthians 12:7-11, clearly teaches that all of the Gifts are for everyone that is born again and filled with the Holy Spirit with the evidence of speaking in tongues. Then we go to verses 28-31, in which we are now talking about Offices and we read clearly not all are Apostles, Prophets, etc. and not all have the Office of Tongues. Again, I want to point out in this passage, it is clearly talking about Offices and not Gifts.

The Office of Tongues is in manifestation such as in a Church service. The Holy Spirit directs the Church to be silent and then someone that is in the Office of Tongues raises their voice in the Heavenly Language and the someone who is in the Office of Interpretation of Tongues raises their voice after the message in tongues and gives God's interpretation. You see this teaching of the order of Ministerial Tongues (the Office of Tongues) in a Church service, as well as, see there is an Office of Tongues that is similar, but not the Gift of Tongues by reading I Corinthians 14:5; 27, 28.

The Gift of Discerning of Spirits Versus the Office of Discerning of Spirits

The Gift of Discerning of Spirits is the ability to manifest all of a person's physical senses in the Spirit world. For instance to see, hear, feel, taste, and smell in the Spirit world. However, most of the time there will only be one of the senses in operation; such as seeing.

The Office of Discerning of Spirits is really the Office of a Prophet. Quite often in the Old Testament a Prophet was referred to as a Seer. The Hebrew word for, "Seer" used in the Old Testament is, "chozeh". Chozeh's full meaning is: a beholder of visions; prophet, seer, gazer. A Prophet lives with the ability to see in the spirit, as I said with the other Gifts. A millionaire has a million dollars, another person may have 10 dollars, but that does not make him a millionaire.

Also, with the Office of Discerning of Spirits (the Office of a Prophet); God initiates the ability and it is more amplified, clearer, it even seems to be a natural appearance, it is so amplified. When God initiates this Gift, it is hard to convince one's natural senses that they are not actually seeing in the natural, a spiritual being or encounter.

Looking at the Gift of Discerning of Spirits

In I Corinthians 12:1-11, as taught in Chapter 5 under the subtitle: Old Strong Tradition, you can plainly see that the Gift of Discerning of Spirits is given to every person to profit withal (V.7). And the Holy Spirit gives to every person, severally as the person is willing or desires (V.11).

In Chapter 5, I go into great depths giving a lot of Scriptures to validate every one that is born again and filled with the Holy Spirit can receive this Gift. Scriptures such as John 17:20-22, where Jesus prayed that we would have the same reputation that He had; and we now have it, as Jesus always got His prayers answered.

And in Philippians 2:5, God clearly invites us to have the same mind that Jesus had. If Jesus was in the presence of any person, He could see if there was a demon spirit that was causing a problem in their body or life.

The Office of Discerning of Spirits or the Office of a Prophet

First of all, look at Ephesians 4:8-12 and I Corinthians 12:28 and you can see that God has set in the Church, "Prophets".

The Office of Discerning of Spirits is the Office of a Prophet. A Prophet will primarily see into the Spirit world. As I mentioned earlier in the Old Testament, a Prophet is co-equally called and rendered as a Seer; they see into the Spirit world. The Prophet will have at *least* two revelation Offices,which would be: the Office of the Word of Wisdom; the Office of the Word of Knowledge and the Office of Discerning of Spirits.

When the Office of the Word of Wisdom is in operation, the Prophet will have insight, perception into the future of people, things or places.

When the Office of the Word of Knowledge is in operation, the Prophet will have insight, perception into the past or present concerning people, things or places.

When the Office of Discerning of Spirits is in operation, the Prophet will have the ability to exercise at least one of the natural senses; duplicated in the Spirit world. For instance, using one's spiritual eyes or ears in the Spirit world.

However, a Prophet will always have in their life predominately the Office of Discerning of Spirits; which is primarily seeing in the Spirit world. And that is why they are called a, "Seer", they see things supernaturally.

When the Office of a Prophet is in operation, the Prophet will see into the Spirit world, much like the Gift of Discerning of Spirits. However, in the Office of a Prophet or you could say the Office of Discerning of Spirits, things seen are clearer, more amplified, made easier in operation. It may sound greater and better by me saying what I am about to say, "but it is not". When the Gift is in operation, a person initiates it (as God has already initiated the Gift to be in operation for every human being, II Peter 1;3,4); but when the Office is in operation, God initiates it. When the Gift is in operation, the person with the Gift has to spend some time concentrating and focusing on the Gift, sometimes it may take a few minutes. When the Office is in operation, it comes instantly. When the Office is in operation, it seems to be more real, as it is more amplified. For instance, if it is the seeing manifestation; the natural eyes think they are seeing it. If it is the hearing manifestation; the natural ears thinks they are hearing it, but the natural eyes and ears really are not hearing and seeing. This has happened to me many times and I am amazed that the people at my side did not hear or see what I just did.

Let me go back and expound on the importance of the Gift versus the Office. They are equally important. It is sort of like food versus water. What is more important? Water is if it is the most needed and food is if it is the most needed. The way I conduct myself in being an instrument for the Lord is of this order: If the Office is not initiated by God, then I imitate the Gift. This is in perfect Godly order. The

Lord knows which one needs to be in manifestation, so He directs us according to the desires of our heart (Psalm 37:4). If I have a desire for people to be blessed, and the Office is not initiated, then God knows I will listen to my heart and initiate the Gift. The novice that is observing the manifestation of the Office or the Gift, does not know the difference. I am simply sharing the difference so people can allow the Gifts of God to be in operation. Many people that flow with the Office will not initiate the Gift because they think it is out of order because of not knowing the truth and direction of God's Word. God wants people to be blessed and the body of Christ is the means for people being blessed. If they know more of the things of God that will cause them to be better instruments, humanity will be more blessed and the Supernatural of God will bring huge masses into the kingdom of God. And YES, both the Gift and the Office are extremely God ordained and Divinely Supernatural!

Let's Look at Some Bible Examples of the Office

Daniel 10:5: "Then I lifted up mine eyes, and looked, and behold a certain man clothed in linen, whose loins were girded with fine gold of Uphaz: V.6. His body also was like the beryl, and his face as the appearance of lightning, and his eyes as lamps of fire, and his arms and his feet like in color to polished brass, and the voice of his words like the voice of a multitude. V.7. And I Daniel alone saw the vision: for the men that were with me saw not the vision..."

Acts 9:3: "And as he journeyed, he came near Damascus: and suddenly there shined round about him a light from heaven: V.4. And he fell to the earth, and heard a voice saying unto him, Saul, Saul, why persecutes thou me? V.5. And he said, Who are thou, Lord? And the Lord said, I am Jesus whom thou persecutest: it is hard for thee to kick against the pricks. V.6. And he trembling and astonished said, Lord, what wilt thou have me to do? V.7. And the men which journeyed with him stood speechless, hearing a voice, BUT SEEING NO MAN."

II Kings 6: 8-17, gives a very good description of the Office of Discerning of Spirits.

Syria was warring against Israel and every time the Syrian king would set up a battle plan to destroy God's people, Elisha would see into the Spirit world and actually set in the Syrian king's secret counsel in which the battle plans were discussed. Of course, the Syrian king nor the secret counsel saw or knew of the Prophet's presence.

The Syrian king, being very upset, thought there was a traitor among his secret counsel. However, one of his servants said, "None, my lord, O king but Elisha the prophet that is in Israel, telleth the king of Israel the words that thou speakest in thy bedchamber". Then it was told the king that Elisha was in Dothan; so the Syrian king sent horses, and chariots, and a great host by night and compassed the city about.

Then Elisha's servant rose early and saw the host compassed about the city with horses and chariots. And the servant said to Elisha, "Alas, my master! What are we going to do?" Elisha saw in the Spirit world and was not troubled, knowing the Spirit world of God's Angelic host is more powerful than anything this natural world could possibly array. Elisha saw in the Spirit world that Dothan was surrounded by God's host of warring angels and that Supernatural, superseded the Syrian army.

When you believe in the Supernatural Gifts and Callings of God and allow them to operate in your life; you have a

Supernatural peace and confidence that you have the victory and it does not matter in the least what the natural world or the natural sensibilities are saying. The devil is limited but we are not!

Notice, as you read this passage, that the Prophet of God saw in the Spirit world when others could not. As you read, you find that Elisha prayed that his young servant would see also, and he was able to see, and this Supernaturally assured him.

Jesus Seeing Nathanael

In John 1:46-49, we find the story of Nathanael being very critical against Jesus, not believing Jesus could be of any value. However, when Jesus told Nathanael that He saw Nathanael under a fig tree, this totally changed Nathanael's opinion instantly. It was very apparent that Jesus saw something that day that was very secretive, very confidential to Nathanael as he was under that fig tree and Nathanael was totally unaware of Jesus' presence.

This Supernatural experience of the Office of Discerning of Spirits caused Nathanael to KNOW that Jesus was the Son of God and Nathanael became a disciple of Jesus because of this Office being in operation. The Gifts and Offices of the Holy Spirit will totally change people's lives for good!

Jesus said in verse 48: "I saw"; notice this phrase is the Greek word, "eido". The fuller meaning of this Greek word is: be aware, look on. "Eido" is equivalent to the Greek word, "optanomai". Optanomai's fuller meaning has these words: to gaze, that is with wide open eyes, as at something remarkable; *discern clearly mentally; to experience, appear, see, perceive.*

As the Office of Discerning of Spirits was in operation, Jesus Supernaturally experienced and clearly saw something that others did not experience or see at all.

3

DOCTRINAL PROOF

Fifty six times in the New Testament, the Greek word, "optanomai" appears. Optanomai's fuller meaning is *to discern clearly, mentally, experience, with wide open eyes, as at something remarkable; appear, look, see, shew self, to discern clearly (physically or mentally); to experience; to appear:—behold, perceive, see, take heed.*

The Greek word, "optanomai" is used in reference to different types of visions, as you can tell by the fuller meaning of the word. However, it is definitely used in reference to a person initiating a vision that is based upon God's Word. I'll give a few verses that clearly display this truth.

There are different types of visions throughout the Scriptures, however, I want to focus on the type of vision in which a person initiates seeing in the Spirit world.

The Greek word, "optanomai" is used quite often in validating this experience. Let me give you some of these Scriptures:

Matthew 5:8: "Blessed are the pure in heart: for they shall see (optanomai) God."

(Note: If our hearts are pure there are times we need to initiate seeing Jesus by our sides. The Bible plainly teaches us that He will never leave us nor forsake us (Hebrew 13:5).

There are different kinds of visions in which God initiates. However, there is a type of vision as mentioned here that is very important for children of God to initiate. In fact, the Hebrew word for this kind of vision is mentioned in Proverbs 29:18: "Where there is no vision the people perish: but he that keepeth the law, happy is he." The word, "vision" in this passage is the Hebrew word, "chazon". This Hebrew word is pronounced, "khaw-zone". The fuller meaning of this word is: *a sight, (mentally), that is, a dream, revelation, or oracle: vision, to gaze at; mentally to perceive, contemplate (with pleasure); specially to have a vision of: behold, look, prophesy, provide, see.)*

Notice in Proverbs 29:18 the word, "law" is the Hebrew word, "torah" which clearly throughout the Scriptures is rendered as, God's commands or God's Word.

So again, we see another passage in the Holy Scriptures teaching, validating, "we can have visions and should".

I will teach in greater depths about Proverbs 29:18 in Chapter 6.

(Note: This is the most God ordained, and is the highest order of visions; as God said we will perish if we do not have them. From a sensibility standpoint, we have a strong tendency to promote visions that our natural sensibilities can relate to as more supernatural, more spiritual. The only time Jesus ever visited me in the natural flesh was October 5th, 1979, at a minister's convention. I give more details of this experience in my book, "Why Jesus Appears to People Today". This was an awesome experience, and I will never forget it. And I would love to have more of these types of experiences. However, from a Scriptural standpoint, the self initiating daydream or vision is the most important and we can have as many of these per day as we like.)

Jesus said in Matthew 22:29, that if we do not know the

Scriptures we err, not knowing the power of God. We could say in reference to Matthew 22:29, if we do not know, accept the teaching of Proverbs 29:18 we err, not knowing the power of God.

In John 1:50, Nathanael's life was totally changed because Jesus initiated seeing him. And it was true. The Greek root word for, "saw" in this passage is, "optomahee."

John 3:36, Jesus said in this passage, "He that believeth on the Son hath everlasting life: and he that believeth not the Son shall not see (optomahee) life; but the wrath of god abideth on him."

Did you notice the clear teaching of Jesus, letting us know those that believe not have no visions, clearly indicating those that believe do or can have optomahee visions.

(Note: The word, "God" in this passage is the Greek word, "theos". Theos is also translated in the New Testament approximately 12 times as god or magistrate. In this passage, "god" is the accurate translation).

John 16:16, Jesus let us know that we can (optomahee) see him after He rose from the dead: "A little while, and ye shall not see me: and again, a little while, and ye shall see (optomahee) me, because I go to the Father."

More Validity

In my book, "Mystery of the Ages" I give over 700 verses just in the New Testament that validates that God has already given us all things that pertain to this life and God-likeness (II Peter 1:3,4). Therefore, God has already given us the ability to, "have visions". Seven hundred verses makes for an extremely strong doctrine of God.

The Gift of Discerning Of Spirits

I Corinthians 12:7 tells us plainly: "But the manifestation of the Spirit is given to every man (the Greek word for, "man" is, "hekastos", and this Greek word is also translated as: any, each one, every one, woman) to profit withal."

Then in verses 8 through 10, God explains what the manifestations are that are given to everyone; which are the Gifts of the Holy Spirit. In verse 10, the Gift of Discerning of Spirits is mentioned. The Greek word for, "discerning" simply says to, "discern". However, most English dictionaries will give the full meaning of the word as: to distinguish someone or something with difficulty by sight or with other senses.

As you study the Gift of Discerning of Spirits throughout the Scriptures you find it is a person that uses one or more of their natural senses duplicated in the Spirit world. For example: we have natural eye sight, so if I use my spiritual eye, I would see something spiritually. I will teach more on this in the Chapter 6, "How to See in the Spirit".

While we are right here in Chapter 12, I want to clarify that God wants everyone to have all of the Gifts of the Holy Spirit. As you noticed in the introduction of the teaching of the Gifts of the Holy Spirit (verse 7), the manifestation of the Spirit is given to everyone. Clearly, the manifestation of the Spirit is the Gifts of the Holy Spirit as that is the teaching for the immediate next three verses for they speak only about the Gifts of the Holy Spirit.

Then the closing of this teaching is in verse 11: "But all these worketh that one and the selfsame Spirit, *dividing* to every *man* severally *as he will*." (Note: The italicized word, "dividing" is the Greek word,"diaireo". This Greek word is also translated as: *distribute*; which is the correct translation

21

based on over 700 verses just in the New Testament. As well as, this is the ONLY passage in the Bible that appears that a person only gets one Gift, and there cannot be a doctrine of God if there is only one passage of Scripture to validate it.

The italicized phrase, "as he will" is the single Greek word, "boulomai". Boulomai does not have the word, "man" in it at all, neither is there any word within the full meaning of this word that could possibly be in reference to the word, "man" or of God saying this. The fuller meaning of the word, "boulomai" is: *be willing, be disposed, minded, be, of own will.*

And the word, "man" in this verse is the Greek word, "hekastos", which is also translated as: each or every; any, one, every (man, one, woman).

Accurately, verse 11 is translated as: "But all these worketh that one and the selfsame Spirit, *distributing* to every *person* severally *as that person is willing*."

Now let's look at verses 8-10 to get the accurate understanding of these verses saying, "for to one," etc.

V.8: "*For to one* is given by the Spirit the Word of Wisdom; *to another* the Word of Knowledge by the same Spirit; V.9. *To another* Faith by the same Spirit; to another the gifts of Healing by the same Spirit; V.10. *To another* the Working of Miracles; *to another* Prophecy; *to another* Discerning of Spirits; *to another* Divers Kinds of Tongues; *to another* the Interpretation of Tongues:

(Note: The italicized phrase, "For to one" in verse 8 is the Greek word, "hos he ho". This Greek word is translated as: *one another* and the word, "For to" is not in this Greek word at all, neither are there any words within this word that could possibly be in reference to the word, "For to".

In verse 8, the italicized phrase, "to another" is the Greek word, "allos". This Greek word is translated as: *one anoth-*

22

er or more and the word, "to" is not in this Greek word at all, neither are there any words within this Greek word that could possibly be in reference to the word, "to".

(Note: In verse 9, the italicized phrase, "To another" is the Greek word, "heteros" and in verse 10, the underlined italicized phrase, "to another" is the same Greek word, "heteros". This Greek word, does not have the word, "to" within its full meaning at all, neither are there any words, within this Greek word, that could possibly be in reference to the word, "to". Heteros is translated as: next or *one another*.)

(Note: All of the other italicized phrases, "to another" in verse 10 are the single Greek word, "allos"; this Greek word does not have the word, "to" within it at all, neither are there any words within this Greek word that could possibly be in reference to the word, "to". This Greek word is translated as: else, more, or *one another*.)

Accurately, verses 8-10 are translated: V.8. "*For one another* is given by the Spirit the Word of Wisdom; *one another* the Word of Knowledge by the same Spirit; V.9. *One another* faith by the same Spirit; to another the Gifts of Healing by the same Spirit; V.10. *One another* the Working of Miracles; *one another* Prophecy; *one another* Discerning of Spirits; *one another* Divers Kinds of Tongues; *one another* the Interpretation of Tongues".

The conclusion of I Corinthians 12:7-11, is the doctrinally correct statement: All of the Gifts of the Holy Spirit are given to every human person, and they will be in operation in the person as they get their will in agreement with God's will, which is His Word.

More Validation

In John 17:20-22, Jesus prayed that God would give us the same reputation that He had. Keep in mind, that Jesus always had His prayers answered. So we now have the same reputation of holiness, perfection, the power of God, and the ability to see in the Spirit world as we will.

John 17:20: "Neither pray I for these alone, but for them also which shall believe on me through *their word.*" (Note: The italicized phrase, "their word" is the Greek word, "logos". The word, "logos" does not have the word, "their" within it at all, neither are there any words with the meaning of the word, "logos" that could possibly be in reference to the word, "their". Logos is also translated as: The Divine Expression (that is Christ); word.

Verse 22: "And the glory (the Greek word for, "glory" is, "Doxa" and the fuller meaning of the word, "doxa" is the, "reputation of God") which thou gavest me I have given them; that they may be one, even as we are one."

John 14:12: "Verily, verily, I say unto you, He that believeth on me, the works that I do shall he do also; and greater works than these shall he do; because I go unto my Father." (Note: The word, "works" both times in this passage is the Greek word, "ergon". This Greek word is also translated as: effort or occupation, act, deed, doing).

So everything that Jesus did, we can do also. Jesus was God in the flesh (John 1:1,14), and at anytime God wants to see in the Spirit world, He can and He does; and now we have that same ability and privilege.

I Cor. 6:17: "But he that is joined to the Lord is one Spirit."

When we accept Jesus Christ as our Lord and Savior, we become one with him (Note: The previous passage, John

17:20-22, as well as many other passages throughout the Bible declaring the same thing).

Being one with Jesus, we then can do anything He did or does.

I John 4:17: "...as He is so are we in this world."

Ephesians 1:22: "And hath put all things under his feet, and gave him to be the head over all things to the Church, V.23. Which is his body, the fullness of him that filleth all in all." (Note: The Greek word for, "filleth" in this passage is, "pleroo" and is also translated as: execute (an office), finish (a period or task), accomplish).

If we are of the fullness of Christ, then we can do everything that He did and does today; so we have the ability to see in the Spirit world as the need arises.

God the Father gave all power and authority to Jesus and Jesus turned around and gave to the Church (which is born again believers); to execute the office of Jesus and to finish the work of God in this world.

4

DOCTRINES OF MAN MAKES GOD'S WORD OF NONE EFFECT

Intro: In this chapter, I want to show how important it is that we never exalt anything above the Word of God. Many people have missed great blessings of God by exalting knowledge, evidence of what sensibilities say, or other supernatural experiences above God's Word.

In Psalm 138:2, the Bible says that God magnifies His Word above His Name.

If God exalts His Word above Himself, then we need to do the same thing.

In Isaiah 55:8, the Bible says, "For my thoughts are not your thoughts, neither are your ways my ways, saith the Lord."

If we want to be everything that God's Word says we can be; if we want everything that God's Word says we can have; we must exalt, magnify God's Word above everything else. We must exalt God's Word above everything our sensibilities have told us. We must exalt God's Word over traditions of mankind. We must understand that God's ways, His intelligence is above ours; His intelligence is superior to ours.

In Proverbs 14:12 and 16:25 the Bible says, "There is a way which seemeth right unto a man, but the end thereof are the ways of death."

We must not go by what seems right, we MUST go by what is right; which is God's Word.

In II Corinthians 10:3 the Bible clearly lets us know that we are at war. As you study this passage, as well as many Scriptures throughout the Bible, you easily understand that our war is with satan and his demons.

As you study verse 5, you can see that a great part of warring with satan is that we cast down imaginations and everything that exalts itself above the knowledge of God.

Clearly, satan's kingdom will war strongly with Christians using sensible knowledge, knowledge that religious traditions have cherished for many ages, to keep them from operating in the Gifts of the Holy Spirit. The Gifts of the Holy Spirit bring huge numbers of people into the kingdom of God.

I used to conduct Church services and crusades without flowing in the Gifts of the Holy Spirit. The crowds were much smaller and the salvations were very few. After I started flowing in the Gifts of the Holy Spirit, the crowds grew tremendously larger and the salvations increased from sometimes 10 per year to as many as 60,000 in one service.

We see the same thing in Peter's life. Off the top of my head, I cannot think of one convert from Peter's ministry until he was filled with the Holy Spirit and operated in the Gifts of the Holy Spirit. His first sermon after being filled with the Holy Spirit with the evidence of speaking in tongues, 3,000 were saved (read Acts 2:1-41).

Notice Peter's second sermon, after he was filled with the Holy Spirit with the evidence of speaking in tongues, and flowed with the Gifts of the Holy Spirit. A man that was paralyzed from birth (Acts 3:1-7; 4:22) was healed so completely that he began to <u>leap and praise God</u>. Notice after the flowing of the Gifts of the Holy Spirit and Peter's sermon there were about 5,000 men saved (not counting the women and children).

When you begin to see demons inside people's bodies as the root of a sickness or a disease, and you cast it out and they are healed instantly, it will draw GREAT attention to the Lord and many will be saved. There is such a Supernatural undeniable atmosphere of God's presence when the Gifts of the Holy Spirit are in operation.

The Gifts of the Holy Spirit are the dinner bell to the Gospel. The operation of the Gifts of the Holy Spirit validates God's Word as truth and places deposits of Eternal Divinity in people's hearts; and they yearn to be born again by accepting Jesus Christ as their Lord and Savior.

Limiting God

Psalm 78:41 says: "Yea, they turned back and tempted God; and limited the Holy One of Israel."

To better understand this statement it is important to consider some other Scriptures.

Look at Isaiah 40:12: "Who hath measured *the waters* in the hollow of his hand, and meted out heaven with the span, and comprehended the dust of the earth in a measure, and weighed the mountains in scales, and the hills in a balance?"

(Note: The italicized phrase, "the waters" is the single Hebrew word, "mayim". This Hebrew word clearly is rendered as "waters". This tells me that God can measure all the waters in existence with the palm of His hand.)

Think about this. If you were to take a U.S. coin called a

quarter and placed it in the center of the United States, that would be the same comparison of placing our solar system (which is our planet earth, the sun, the moon and all of the other planets in our solar system, such as Mars, Jupiter, etc.) in the middle of the Milky Way Galaxy. Now understand that there are over 300 million other solar systems within our Milky Way Galaxy. Then understand that there are many more galaxies than we have the capability of seeing. Now think of all the water upon the earth, then our galaxies and all of the other galaxies. And God measures ALL THE WATERS IN THE PALM OF HIS HAND. GOD IS A BIG GOD!

Clearly, we can understand His power. He never got off of His throne and He spoke the worlds (Notice: worlds, not world) with the power of His Word (Hebrews 11:3).

Now think back on our leading verse "Psalm 78:41"; God's people limited Him. In Numbers 13:32, clearly the Bible tells us how they limited God. They had an evil report. If you will read Numbers 13:1, 2, the Lord told the children of Israel that He *had given them* the land of Canaan.

Then in 13:32, clearly the Bible tells us they brought up an evil report.

In Chapters 13 and 14 you will see clearly that God's people limited God because they refused to believe Him; instead they believed what their eyes and sensibilities said. They exalted the knowledge of sensibilities above the knowledge of God and this limited God. Hebrews 4:5, 6 tells us the same thing; they entered not into God's rest. They entered not into the promise land that God said was theirs, because of unbelief (Note: The Greek word for, "unbelief" is, "apapeitheia". This Greek word is also translated as: rebellious, disobedience, unpersuadable). God's people knew the Word of God, but God could not persuade them to act on it; and it limited the Huge, Almighty God.

God is a God of integrity. He will not honor anything but His Word. And He has not changed, if we want God's blessings we must believe Him, and believing His Word is believing God.

The Truth is True Today

In Matthew 15:6, Jesus clearly made the statement that the commandments of God are made none effect because of people exalting their traditions above God's Word (His commandments).

Today, this truth is still prevalent. People exalt what religious leaders have taught, over the Word of God. And that is why they do not have the Gifts of the Holy Spirit operating in their lives. As well as, the religious leaders that exalt their religions, seemingly good doctrine; they also have not the Gifts of the Holy Spirit operating in their lives.

Just because a religious organization is large does not mean that it is right. The same is true in regards to a large Church. Hell is big. I am not saying all big Churches are in religious traditions. It makes no difference if the Church is big or small, we must not exalt any teaching above God's Word.

Many years ago, I was setting in a minister's meeting in which Brother John Osteen; Pastor of Lakewood Church in Houston, Texas, was conducting. He said for years his Church was very small and it bothered him. He said he would always jog every morning, and one morning he was jogging a great distance from home and twisted his ankle real bad. He said he could no longer run and only hobbled back home. He said the more he tried to walk with that twisted ankle the bigger it got. As he was nearing home, he said he heard God speak to him. God said, "John, I want you to look at your ankle and tell me, John, is bigger better?"

God's Word is not truth because of a lot of big things proving it. God's Word is truth because it's God's Word. We must have the mind set as Romans 3:4, which says: "....Yea, let God be true, but every ***man*** ***a liar;***...." (Note: The Greek word for the italicized word, "man" is, "anthropos". This Greek word is also accurately translated as: human being. And the underlined italicized phrase, "a liar" is the Greek word, "pseustes". This Greek word is also translated as: falsifier, and untruth or attempt to deceive by falsehood).

Old Strong Tradition

Since birth, I've gone to Full Gospel Churches and I've heard this doctrine preached, taught, and believed by Full Gospel people all of my life. This false doctrine has crippled the Church of the Lord Jesus Christ in a huge way. This false doctrine has kept the Church extremely weak and defeated for so many years.

This false doctrine has kept people from allowing the Supernatural to flow in their lives and in their Churches.

This false doctrine seems so humble and seems so right. However, this false doctrine has ONLY one passage in the whole Bible to validate it; and as you study the Bible it is very clear that we need at LEAST 2-3 clear passages of Scripture to validate a doctrine of God (Notice: Matthew 18:16: "...***that in the mouth*** of two ***or*** three ***witnesses*** every ***word*** may be established." (Note: The first italicized phrase is the single Greek word, "stoma"). Stoma is also translated as: ***language***. Also notice the italicized word, "or", which is the Greek word, "e". This Greek word is also translated as: *but rather, than indeed*. The italicized word, "witnesses" is the Greek word, "martus". Martus is also translated as: *record*. The italicized word, "word" is the Greek word, "rhema", which is also translated as: the spoken word, a matter or topic, *command*). To make this portion of Matthew 18:16 more accurately translated would be: "...that every command of God, every doctrine of God is established by two but rather, indeed by three records, which would be passages of Scripture."

We see this same truth written in: I Corinthians 14:29; II Corinthians 13:1; Numbers 35:30; Deuteronomy 17:6, 19:15; Psalm 12:6; Hebrews 10:28; John 8:17.

So misinterpretation of I Corinthians 12:7-11, cannot be a doctrine of God, as it is only one passage in the WHOLE BIBLE.

However, in our modern Bibles today, it is written to SEEM like the Gifts of the Holy Spirit are very limited to having only one Gift. I've noticed wherever this doctrine is practiced there are very few that have even one Gift; and in those same places, it is EXTREMELY rare for a demonstration of any Gift. And if so, there is only the demonstration of only the Gift of Ministerial Tongues and the Gift of Interpretation.

Old, Old Man Made Doctrine

The misinterpretation of I Corinthians 12:7-11, has crippled the Church on a world-wide scale. Let's examine this passage to find the truth of what the Holy Spirit wants us to know.

Verse 7 is the introduction of the Gifts of the Holy Spirit and this verse is extremely overlooked by those that believe people can have only one Gift and sometimes two (if you are really Spiritual?????) Notice the introduction of the Gifts of the Holy Spirit and the closing clearly lets us know that all of the Gifts of the Holy Spirit are for all people (of course, that are born again and filled with the Holy Spirit with the evidence of speaking in tongues). Looking at verse 7 the introduction of the Gifts of the Holy Spirit: V.7: "But the manifestation of the Spirit is GIVE TO EVERY MAN to profit withal." (Note: In verse 7 and 11 the word, "man" is the Greek word, "hekastos". This Greek word is also translated as each one, woman or man). And of course, it is plain to understand what the manifestation that is given to everyone is as you read on in verses 8-10, which are all of the Gifts of the Holy Spirit.

Then we see this same truth in verse 11, validating again that all of the Gifts of the Holy Spirit are given to everyone. Let's read verse 11: "But all these worketh that one and the selfsame Spirit, *dividing* to every man severally *as he will*." First of all, I want to point out that as you study English grammar the italicized word, "he" cannot jump backward over man, to refer to Spirit. "He" must refer to "man". But a greater truth to validate that the Gifts of the Holy Spirit are given to everyone is the fact the italicized phrase, "*as he will*" is the Greek word, "boulomai". This Greek word does not have the word, "he" within it at all, neither are there any words within this word that could possibly be in reference to the word, "he". Boulomai is also translated as: *be willing, be minded, choose or prefer, to wish, desire, please).* The italicized word, "dividing" is the **Greek** word, "diaireo". Diaireo is also translated as: *distribute.*

The accurate translation of verse 11, would be: "But all these worketh that one and the selfsame Spirit, *distributing* to every *person* severally *as desires.*"

Again, the introduction and the closing of the teaching of the Gifts of the Holy Spirit validate that ALL of the Gifts of the Holy Spirit is for all people.

But what do we do with verses 8-10 that appear so clearly that a person only gets one Gift?

No. 1. Anytime a passage in the Bible does not agree with the rest of the Bible; something is wrong. I find in my studies that it is a mistranslation. We must keep in mind, that all of our modern day Bibles are either versions from a translation or a translation from the original languages that the Bible was written in. No. 2. We need to look at the original language of the Bible and see if the original language had other words within it that are co-equal with proper translation. For instance, as I said before, you can take the English word, "person" and it can refer to a man or a woman. We must take the word, "person" and look at the context of the book or the letter to determine if it is referring to man or woman. Every language has these same truths. No. 3. The translators, at times, assumed a word should be translated and there are obvious times they were wrong).

A good example of translators making a wrong translation is Romans 8:16: "The Spirit *itself* beareth witness with our spirit, that we are the children of God." (Note: The italicized word, "itself" is the Greek word, "autos". Autos is also translated as: *him, himself*. And of course the word, "himself" is the accurate translation; the Holy Spirit is not an "it".

Let's read verses 8-10 in I Corinthians 12:8: "*For to one* is given by the Spirit the Word of Wisdom; *to another* the Word of Knowledge by the same Spirit; V.9. *To another* Faith by the same Spirit; *to another* the Gifts of Healing by the same Spirit; V.10. *To another* the Working of Miracles; *to another* Prophecy; *to another* Discerning of Spirits; to another Divers Kinds of Tongues; *to another* the Interpretation of Tongues:"

(Note: The first italicized phrase in verse 8, "***For to one***" is the single Greek word, "hos he ho"; this Greek word does not have the words, "For to" in it at all. This Greek word, "hos he ho" is translated as, "***One another***". And this is the correct translation that agrees with the rest of the Bible.)

(Note: The second italicized phrase in verse 8, "***to another***" is the Greek word, "allos". This Greek word is also translated as: ***one another.*** This Greek word, "allos" is also the exact same Greek word for the second phrase, "to another" in verse 9 and the exact Greek word for the phrase "to another" in verse 10 every place except the 4th time it is written in verse 10 and that Greek word for the 4th time the phrase, "to another" is rendered is the Greek word, "heteros" and this Greek word is also translated as, "***one another***".)

By staying in context with the rest of the Bible and accurately translating from the Greek, these verses are translated:

V.8: "***For to one another*** is given by the Spirit the Word of Wisdom; ***to one another*** the Word of Knowledge by the same Spirit; V.9. ***To one another*** Faith by the same Spirit; ***to one another*** the Gifts of Healing by the same Spirit; V.10. ***To one another*** the Working of Miracles; ***to one another*** Prophecy; ***to one another*** Discerning of Spirits; ***to one another*** Divers Kinds of Tongues; ***to one another*** the Interpretation of Tongues:"

5

FAITH AND IMAGINATION

Intro: Should Christians use their imagination?

For so many years cults, occults and other false religions have talked about imaginations and used the teachings that deal with the imaginations so much that Christians have almost totally abandoned the thought of using their imaginations.

However, just because there is something that is similar to that which is Godly, I am not going to stop believing and using the Godly. A good example is liquid; God ordained that humans should drink liquids, if we do not, we will die. Just because satan has inspired people to take water (liquid) and use it to make evil liquids; I am not going to stop drinking water. In like manner, satan has perverted imaginations; the Bible calls them vain imaginations. And Christians are dying spiritually because they refuse to use their imaginations for God.

We never have to be afraid that we are going to get into error as long as we have plenty of good, sound, clear Scriptures to validate our beliefs and our practices.

Many Christians are afraid of using their imaginations, *equating it with evil*. But God surely had a reason to make mankind with an imagination.

Bible Examples

God ordained humanity to use their imaginations from the very beginning.

Reading Genesis 11:6: "And the Lord said, Behold the people is one, and they have all one language; and this they begin to do: and now nothing will be restrained from them which they have *imagined* to do." (Note: God said this! This tells me that any evil thing that these Godless people would imagine to do, would happen. It is because of the Supernatural Ordination of Imagination that God set in order).

As you read on in this chapter, God stopped them, because He knew they were living evil, ungodly lives.

However, a strong point that I want to make is the fact that we have a better covenant established upon better promises (Hebrews 7:19-22; 8:6). If that is not true, then Jesus did not need to come to this earth and die on a cruel cross; we then do not need the New Testament. However, Jesus came and He died, not in vain, and we have a New Covenant established upon better promises. So whatever God did for anyone of the Old Testament, He will do for us today and more! So how much more can we as born again, Spirit-filled Christians use our imaginations and glorify God and bless people! Our imaginations will be to glorify God and to bless people. Our imaginations will be founded upon EXACTLY what God's Word says! Doing the works of Jesus and greater (John 14:12-14), which is opening the blinded eyes, opening the deaf ears, causing the crippled to walk, seeing the incurable cured, recreating bodily parts (Matthew 15:30, Jesus healed the maimed.) The word, "maimed" in most dictionaries will say, "those missing bodily parts". The Greek simply says, "maimed".

This is exactly what I do in experiencing miracles. I visualize what the Bible says as I release God's anointing in people's lives. For example, if a person is blind, I see them seeing with perfection; and the list goes on in each case; I see the dead rise, and they rise.

Look at Genesis 15:5: "And He brought him forth abroad, and said, **LOOK** now toward heaven, and tell the stars, if thou be able to number them: and He said unto him, so shall thy seed be."

God told Abraham to "count the stars. . . so shall your descendants be." (Note: God was clearly telling Abraham to use his imagination).

The italicized word, "Look" in this passage is the Hebrew word, "nabat". This Hebrew word is also translated as: *to look intently at; by implication to regard with pleasure, consider, regard, see.*

Clearly, God was telling Abram to see with his spiritual eyes (which is using your imagination). Abraham was seeing his descendents as many as the stars of Heaven. And if Jesus Christ is the Lord of your life, you are one of those stars! God was also letting Abraham know that all of his descendents will be stars in the kingdom of God! You are somebody in the mind and heart of God!

Reading Joshua 1:8: "This book of the law shall not depart out of thy mouth: *but thou shalt meditate* therein day and night, that thou mayest observe to do according to all that is written therein: for then thou shalt make thy way prosperous, and then thou shalt have good success." (Note: The italicized phrase is the single Hebrew word, "hagah". This Hebrew word is also co-equally rendered as, "*imagine*").

God was telling Joshua to imagine the Word of God as being truth! We all should have Godly imaginations of God's Word, because it is the highest truth in all of existence.

God told Joshua if he would imagine God's Word day

and night that he would be prosperous and have good success. Joshua did exactly as God had instructed him and he prospered and had good success. Let's look on in this book of Joshua to see what God calls prosperity and good success.

In Joshua 3:13-17, Joshua and the people with him needed to cross the Jordan River during flood stage. In my studies, I find that the Jordan River, at that time, normally was about 50 to 100 feet deep, so it was much deeper at the this time. As you read this passage, you find that the Jordan River separated just like the Red Sea in times past with Moses and the children of Israel.

Looking further on in Joshua 6, God told Joshua that He had given the city of Jericho to him. However, at that time, the city of Jericho had unsurpassable walls around it that protected it. The walls were 34' tall and 34' wide. However, God gave Joshua instruction to march around the walls one time for 6 days and on the 7th day march around it 7 times and have the priest blow their trumpets and the people with Joshua shout, and the walls fell flat. This tells me that the walls were pushed into the ground, because walls 34' tall and 34' wide; if they were to fall over, they would still be 34' tall.

Then reading on in Joshua, Chapter 10, you find the story of Joshua and God's people in battle against the Amorites and it was impossible for Joshua and the children of Israel to avenge themselves with the evening coming. So Joshua spoke openly in front of all Israel and said, "Sun, stand still; moon, stand still." And the sun and the moon stood still about a whole day and Joshua and the Israelites avenged themselves.

As you study from the time that God told Joshua to "IMAGINE" God's Word, day and night until the time that all of these Supernatural miracles took place from Joshua,

Chapter 3 to Chapter 10; was less than one year.

No wonder the devil has fought so hard to keep God's people from using their imaginations for God!

Be Biblical without fear. Take what God has said in His Word, and imagine it that way in your life!

Medical Study Validates Imagination

I was watching one of Sid Roth's T.V. programs and he said there was a study of medical students at a certain medical university that were studying a certain disease and 50% of those students started having symptoms of the very disease they were studying.

What was taking place, was the fact that they were giving a lot of thinking about the disease. They were using their imaginations about the disease, and it affected their natural bodies. They brought something out of the demonic realm into the natural realm by IMAGINATION.

How much more will this law, this truth work for born again, Spirit-filled Christians using their imaginations to bring out of God's Spirit world into our natural world things that are promised in His Word.

Just imagine God's Word as Truth! Proverbs 23:7: "For as he thinketh in his heart so is he." When a person thinks, they are having imaginations. If you think about your car, you can describe it, even if you're on the other side of the world. You are having an imagination with your thinking process. Here in Proverbs, God is telling us plainly that our thinking (our imagination) will produce in the natural world.

Jesus said in Matthew 7:7: "...to seek and you would find." This works both ways. It's simply a law of God, that God has meant for good. However, many people take good things and pervert them. Someone under the influence of satan can SEEK ill will and it will come to them. How much more will the law of God work for someone that is under the influence of God and they SEEK for what God's Word has to say.

God has ordained the human mind to imagine things to bless our lives. As children, we began to imagine accomplishments and they came to pass because we never gave up on our imagination. People have imagined being in many different professions and for those who never lost their imagination it came to pass. We imagine our homes when we are away from home and that's how we find our homes because in our mind's eye we know what it looks like. *These are truths based upon natural knowledge placed in the human mind.*

How much more will SUPERNATURAL KNOWLEDGE, GOD'S WORD, work for us!

Placing God's Word into our minds and thinking about it ✝ equals imagination.

Faith & Imagination

In this subtitle, I want to show you that real Bible faith is imagination.

Let's look at some passages in the Bible that will help us come to this understanding.

In Hebrews 11:1, faith is defined as: "...*evidence of things not seen.*" If it is something you can't see, then it has to deal with the realm of the imagination.

Webster's dictionary says imagine means: *to form a mental image of (something not present).* What could more closely describe the Bible definition of faith in Hebrews 11:1! The people, they talked about in Hebrews, Chapter 11, used their imagination.

Verse 3 is under the heading of verse 1. Verse 1, clearly lets us know that faith and imagination are the same. By looking at verse 3, we can see that God is telling us that He used His imagination to create the worlds. Real Bible imagination is a powerful force that God, Himself, used and uses and He is giving us the privilege to use it also. God ordained imagination has creative power. God ordained imagination in simply imagining what God's Word says as truth. Just imagine God's Word as truth! Because it is!

We can create health, healing, prosperity and bodily parts made whole with the power of imagination. Find many Scriptures that clearly say the same thing, and imagine them as truth. Bring the truth of God's Word out of the Spirit world into the natural world with the power of Godly imagination.

Faith is linked with imagination like wet is linked with water. The two are inseparable. This is why the devil has stirred up such a fuss over this subject. No doubt, one main reason the ***devil inspired eastern religions*** to utilize the imagination was to ***muddy the waters and make Christians afraid it might be wrong***.

Look at the powerful miracles accomplished in the Old Testament because of people using their imagination (their faith):

Hebrews 11:5, Enoch was translated.

V.6. Without imagination (faith) it is impossible to please God.

V.7. By imagination, Noah was warned of God and built an ark.

V.8. By imagination, Abraham, when he was 100 years old, fathered the child that Sarah conceived by him when she was 90 (notice Genesis 17:17 & 21:5).

V.27. By imagination, Moses ***endured as seeing*** Him

who is invisible. (Note: The Greek word for, *"endured"* in the verse is, "kartereo". This Greek word is also translated as: to be *strong, steadfast, patient*). Also, notice the underlined italicized phrase, "as seeing". This is the Greek word, "horao" and has the fuller meaning as: *to discern clearly mentally, to see*.

Just by reading verse 27, you can see that Moses was strong and steadfast and had great Supernatural victories because he used his imagination. (Notice: The only way a person can see into the invisible world is to use their imagination.)

V.29. Moses first imagined the Red Sea parting; and then it did. Again, the miracle working power of imagination brings something out of the Spirit world into the natural world.

V.30. Joshua saw the walls of Jericho down with his imagination; and then it happened in the natural world.

V.32. First by imagination, David seen his little stone going into t.e narrow opening of Giant Goliath's helmet killing him, long before it happened. But it happened! (Notice: I Samuel 17).

V.35. Women of the Old Testament received their dead, but refused death and used their imagination seeing their loved ones alive with their imagination, and their dead raised to life again. Keep in mind, we have a New Covenant today, established upon better promises and everything God did for the people of the Old Testament, He will do for us today and more!

God's Glory By Imagination

By reading II Corinthians, Chapter 3 and Chapter 4,

we can easily understand that God's Glory, His Reputation becomes a natural manifestation and natural reality by a born again, Spirit-filled Christian using their imagination in agreement with God's Word.

Let's examine these chapters: First of all, we need to understand that the words, "glory & glorious" in every verse in Chapters 3 and 4 are the same Greek word, which is, "doxa". The full meaning of the word, "doxa" is: glory, dignity, honor, **_be of reputation_**. (Clearly, doxa is "having the reputation of God"). Doxa is the same Greek word used throughout the New Testament when referring to God's Glory, God's Reputation or Jesus' Glory or His Reputation.

A real good passage to validate this doctrine is in John, Chapter 17, when Jesus was praying for us that we shall believe (that's "we" Christians today). Look at verses 20-22 where Jesus was praying: V.20. "Neither pray I for these alone, but for them also which SHALL BELIEVE on me through *their word*; V.21. That they all may be one; as thou, Father, art in me, and I in thee, that they also may be one in us: that the world may believe that thou hast sent me. V.22. **_And the glory which thou gavest me I have given them...._**" (Note: The italicized phrase in verse 20 is the Greek word, "logos". The fuller meaning of the word, "logos" is: **_The Divine Expression, doctrine, word_**.) (Note: The word, "their" is not within the word, "logos" at all, neither are there any words within this Greek word that could possibly be in reference to the word, "their"). Accurately, this phrase is simply written, "The Divine Word".

Also note that the word, "glory" in verse 22, is the Greek word, doxa; clearly telling us that Jesus had the reputation of God, and absolutely so! However, the awesome good news about this passage is: No.1. Jesus was praying for us today! No.2. Jesus always got His prayers answered as He

44

always prayed, "THE PERFECT WILL OF GOD". No.3. WE NOW HAVE GOD'S REPUTATION!

Now let's go back to II Corinthians, Chapters 3 and 4 understanding EVERY time the words "glory" or "glorious" were written, it is the Greek word, "doxa" being used which is "THE REPUTATION OF GOD".

Verse 3:7 ...Note: Moses had the Reputation of God on his being so strong that his face shined. As you study this experience, you will find that it was so strong that Moses had to cover his face, so the people of the Old Testament could look upon him.

Verses 7 and 13 clearly teach us that the "glory" of the Old Testament is now past away and the "glory" of the New Testament exceeds that of the Old Testament. In verse 10, the fact is brought out that the "glory" of the Old Testament is nothing, compared to the "glory," the Reputation of God for the New Testament people (in which we are!).

Understanding How Doxa is Manifested Today

II Corinthians 3:18: "But we all *with open face* beholding *as in a glass* the glory of the Lord are changed into the same image from glory to glory, *even as by the Spirit* of the Lord." (Let's analyze this verse: The first italicized phrase, "with open" is the Greek word, "anakalupto". This Greek word is also translated as: *"uncovered"* and the underlined italicized word, "face" is the Greek word, "prosopon". This Greek word is also translated as: "person or *vision"*).

Notice the italicized phrase, "as in a glass", which is the Greek word, "katoptrizomai". This Greek word is also translated as: *to mirror oneself, to see reflected, vision.*

And the last italicized phrase, "even as by the Spirit" is

the Greek word, "pneuma". This Greek word is also translated as: Divine, God, Christ's Spirit, the Holy Spirit. (Note: Keep in mind, that you cannot Scripturally separate God, Jesus, the Holy Spirit and the Word of God; as they are all the same). Jesus clearly said in John 6:63: "...the words that I speak *unto you, they are Spirit ...*" (The italicized phrase, "unto you they are Spirit" is the exact Greek word,"pneuma", used in II Corinthians 3:18 in reference to the Holy Spirit.

Making II Corinthians 3:18, real plain and incredibly accurate by translation of the Greek New Testament words and the whole Bible it would read: "But we all *with an open person* beholding *as looking into a mirror* the glory of the Lord are changed into the same image from glory to glory, *even as by the Spirit*, which in the highest order of God's Word."

(Note: *We are changed from God's Reputation into more of God's Reputation as we look into God's Word. Just as we look into a natural mirror every morning and change our appearance, we look into the Word of God and see how God sees us, then accept His opinion and change our person into His Reputation.)*

Read again 3:18 and know this truth: we are using our imagination as we look into God's Word seeing with our imagination God's Glory upon and in our life, spiritually and naturally.

II Corinthians 4:1: "Therefore, seeing we have this ministry... (what ministry? The ministry that Chapter 3 is talking about, "the Glory of the Lord"; the Reputation of God).

V. 3: "But if our Gospel (Good News) be hid, it is hid to them that are lost." V.4: (Note: How is it hid? Read verse 4 for the answer) "In whom the god of this world hath blinded the mind of them, which believe not, least the light of the glorious (Reputation of God) Gospel of Christ, who is the image of God, should shine unto them." (Note: People that do not believe the teaching that the Holy Spirit is making plain in II Corinthians, Chapters 3 and 4 concerning having the very Reputation of God; gives satan liberty to blind their eyes. They just cannot see it!)

The Scriptures that we've been elaborating on in Chapters 3 and 4 are clear concerning God's Reputation for us and how to have it. Now let's look at Chapter 4 in detail to validate this is not just a Spiritual experience. It is clear that this Glory of God is to be made known and experienced in this natural world, in our natural flesh.

In verse 6, notice God is commanding this light, this understanding of the Glory of God to be known to us. This helps us to clearly understand the small cased, "god" of verse 4 is talking about satan. The devil is blinding people so they cannot experience this Glory, but God is COMMANDING it to shine in our lives and hearts.

Where is the Glory to manifest that God is commanding? Read on in verse 7: "We have this treasure in earthen vessels (not Heavenly vessels, but earthen). V.10. .....*that the life* of Jesus made manifest in our body." (Note: The italicized phrase, "that the life" is the Greek word, "zoe", which is translated as: life the way God has it). This validates that we now have the Reputation of God in our earthen vessels (our physical bodies).

V.11: "...the life of Jesus might be made manifest in our mortal flesh." (Note: The word, "life" in this passage is the Greek word, "zoe"; with the Greek meaning of, "life the way God has it").

Summing up clearly what the teaching of Chapter 4:1-11 is primarily talking about, would be said: We have the ministry of God's Reputation, because we believe God's Word. And we have it in our earthen vessels, our bodies, our mortal flesh!

Any time someone repeats something, it is clear that it is important. Not only did God repeat the fact that we NOW have the Reputation of God; He said it 3 different ways, and all of them undeniably in reference to our mortal, natural flesh.

Chapter 3:18, gives us clear instructions how God's Glory would become a reality to us. However, 4:17,18 gives us advanced instructions, after we have believed we have it.

Let's analyze verses 17 & 18: Focusing on our topic, look at the last part of verse 17: ".....God's eternal weight of glory" (God's Reputation). (Note: The statement is made about God's Glory in verse 17 and then verse 18 explains simply how it is brought from the Spiritual into the natural; from the Supernatural realm of God into the temporal realm of humanity.) V. 18: "*While we look* not at the things which are seen, but at the things which are not seen: for the things which are seen are temporal, but the things which are not seen are eternal." (Real clear; looking, seeing in the unseen world is: USING OUR IMAGINATION)! Our imagination is the means of bringing God's Reputation from the Spirit realm, the realm of God into the natural, physical realm. (Note: The italicized phrase, "*While we look*" is the Greek word, "skopeo". This Greek word is comparable to the Greek word, "optanomai". This Greek word is also rendered as: *mentally seeing or mentally having a vision*). Another confirmation: mentally seeing is using your imagination.

The Ephesians Prayer

The Holy Spirit inspired the Apostle Paul to give us this prayer from Ephesians. I pray every day what I believe the Lord wants me to pray from Ephesians 1:16-19 and then

Ephesians 3:14-20. I heard Brother Kenneth Hagin, Sr., say this about 1975. He said, he had been in the ministry for several years and had pastored for about 12 years, when he found this prayer that I now pray. He said, he started praying this prayer every day and sometimes many times per day. Brother Hagin said after a few months he started seeing and understanding things he never saw before. He said, he was surprised the people did not get upset with what he had taught in the past. From the way Brother Hagin said this, it made me think it was like being born again, again. So since then I pray this prayer every day. There have been times that I have not because of emergencies, etc., but primarily I have prayed this prayer every day since about 1975. And I've noticed over the years the Lord showing me things in the Bible that I've read hundreds of times; things that changed my total opinion about doctrine. Today (February 26, 2013), I have about 30-40 books that I am working on that I've never heard one person ever preach about, I've never heard one person talk about. In all of my books that I have in print, most of the information, I've not heard any one teach or talk about it. The Holy Spirit changes us from Glory to Glory, even by His Spirit (II Corinthians 3:18).

Let's analyze Ephesians 1:18: "***The eyes*** of your ***understanding*** being enlightened; that ye may know what is the hope of his calling, and what the riches ***of the glory*** of His inheritance in the saints, V.19. And what is the exceeding greatness ***of his power*** to us-ward who believe, according to the working of His mighty power." (Note: The italicized phrase, "***The eyes***" is the Greek word, "ophthalmos". This Greek word is taken from the Greek word, "optanomai". This Greek word's fuller meaning is: ***to discern clearly, mentally experience, to discern clearly mentally; to experience, perceive, take heed***).

EYE

49

Also notice the italicized word, "understanding", which is the Greek word, "dianoia". This Greek word is also translated as: deep thought, by implication its exercise: *imagination.*

Notice also the italicized phrase "of the glory" is the Greek word, "doxa" which has the fuller meaning of: *God's Reputation.*

The italicized phrase, "of his power" is the Greek word, "dunamis". This Greek word's fuller meaning is: *specifically miraculous power, usually by implication a miracle itself, worker of miracles, mighty wonderful work.*

This Ephesians prayer endorses us to use our imagination of God's Word so that we can bring out of the world of Divinity into our natural world, God's Reputation; his greatest miracle working power for us as Children of God.

6

THE TWO LAWS

When we understand that there are only two laws in existence, it will help us tremendously in having victory in our lives. Knowing this truth is a major key in getting rid of all problems.

Clearly, I will show you from the Scriptures that everything in existence is governed, controlled and made manifest either by God and His angels or by satan and his demons.

There is only the law of life in Christ or the law of sin and death.

Validating the Two Laws

Roman 8:2: "For the law of the Spirit of life in Christ Jesus hath made me free from the law of sin and death."

Clearly, God's Word teaches us there are only two laws in existence, which are God's laws and the kingdom of satan's laws.

Jesus explained this truth, this doctrine in Luke 11:23, 24 (Jesus said): "He that is not with me is against me: and he that gathereth not with me scattereth. V.24. When the unclean spirit is gone out of a man ...." (Note: In verse 23, Jesus clearly lets us know that there are only two laws; that which is for Him and that which is against Him. In verse 24, He clearly explains that the law that is against Him is satanic spirits).

Anything that is not in agreement with God's Word, you can rest assured there is a demon spirit as the root of the problem.

Matthew 12:30, Mark 9:40 and Luke 9:50, also record the same teaching as Luke 11: 23, 24. In Acts 10:38, God also lets us know about the two laws. It reads, "How God anointed Jesus of Nazareth with the Holy Ghost and with power: who went about doing good, and healing all that were oppressed of the devil; for God was with Him."

Plainly, God is calling any sickness as an oppression of the devil!

What About Carnality?

Romans 8:6: "For to be carnally minded is death; but to be Spiritually minded is life and peace. V.8. Because the carnal mind is enmity against God...."

Tradition has horribly crippled the body of Christ by teaching that there are 3 laws. They say, it is either sin (of the devil) or of God or it is just of the flesh. The devil has had great victory because of this lie. The demon spirits of hell have hid in people's bodies and lives because people have not dealt with the source of the problem, which is a demon. Many people have died prematurely because they never dealt with the source of the problem, a demon spirit.

In Romans 8:6, we can see that carnality is death. This is satan's promotion, he comes to kill (John 10:10). And then in verse 7, God plainly tells us that carnality is an enemy

52

against God.

Christians have been defeated by letting a demon live in their body or in their life because of this demonic tradition which says, "it's just of the flesh". The demon says to them when they have a certain desire, problem, sickness or disease, *"it's not of God, that's obvious; however, it is not sin, it is not of the devil; it's just of the flesh"*. And they allow that demon to be a part of their body or a part of their life. And that is the reason they do not get victory over that problem. This allows the lying demon that was in their life to let in a worse demon than what he is. (Notice Matthew 12:45: "Then goeth he, and taketh with himself seven other spirits more wicked than himself and they enter in and dwell there: and the last state of that man is worse than the first..."). "KNOW, if it is not of God, if it is not in agreement with God's Word, there is a demon spirit as the root of the problem, a demon is the source of the problem.

Understand that it is a demon that says, "You're just in the flesh so it's not so bad".

Another False Tradition

This tradition of man, "that Christians cannot have a demon", has been taught all over the world. This is another tradition that has caused many Christians to be defeated in so many areas of their lives.

Of course, Christians cannot be possessed by a demon spirit, that would be impossible. But Christians all over the world get sick. And God calls sickness and disease an oppression of the devil in Acts 10:38. I've been to over 30 different countries as many as 10-15 times in my life, doing miracle crusades and services and I've heard this tradition of man being taught.

James gives us another account validating that Christians can be influenced and oppressed by demonic spirits. Let's read 1:17: "Every good gift and every perfect gift is from above, and cometh down from the Father of lights, with whom there is no variableness, neither shadow of turning."

God is the same yesterday, today and forever (Hebrews 13:8). Anything that is not good, does not come from God. So clearly understanding that there is only one other law, one other source; we can clearly know if it is not good, it is not of God. If it is not good, it is most definitely of the devil.

God never has changed and He never will. He does not vary in the least!

Lamentations also gives us another witness. Let's read 3:38: "Out of the mouth of the most High proceeded not evil and good!"

God never has been the source of any kind of bad or evil and never will!

This is Why the Devil Has Promoted His Lies

I want to show you clearly why the devil wants humanity to think wrong, bad things are just of the flesh and why he wants Christians to think that they cannot be oppressed or influenced or have a demon in their body.

Jesus said if we will understand this truth, this doctrine taught in Mark, Chapter 4, we then will know all of the truths, the doctrines of God and will experience all of God's blessings in His Word.

Let's examine Mark 4:13-20. V.13: "And He said unto them, *KNOW* ye not this *parable*, and how then will ye *KNOW* all *parables*?" (Note: The first italicized word, "know" is the Greek word, "eido"). This Greek word is also translated as: *vision, be aware, have knowledge, be sure, understand*. The second italicized word, *"know"* is the Greek word, "ginosko". This Greek word is also translated as: *allow, feel, have, be resolved, be sure.* The italicized word, "parable" is the Greek word, "parabole". This Greek word is also translated as: proverb (which dictionaries explain as: a simple and *CONCRETE saying* popularly known and repeated which expresses *a TRUTH*, based on common sense or the practical experience of humanity. (Note: Keep in mind, that God's Word is the Highest truth in existence).

Now let's read Mark 4:13, from a simpler and more accurate translation: "And Jesus said unto them, visualize, and have knowledge of this concrete truth of God's Word then you will be able to feel, have and be assured of all of the concrete truths of God's Word."

In essence, if a person will understand this truth that Jesus is explaining from verse 14-20, a person will then be able to experience and know all of the victories of God's Word from Genesis to Revelation!

Let's analyze with simplicity in verse 14-20. No.1. Immediately, after Jesus encouraged us to KNOW this parable, this divine truth; He then says, "The sower soweth the word, and IMMEDIATELY!!! satan comes to take it out of our hearts!" This actually sums up one of the greatest doctrines, one of the most important doctrines of God. Because if you understand this doctrine, YOU WILL EXPERIENCE ALL OF GOD'S WORD, NOT JUST IN YOUR HEAD AND HEART, BUT IN YOUR NATURAL LIFE!!!!!

From verses 15-20, Jesus then explains the different ways that satan and his kingdom come.

This is a huge passage of Scripture that the devil does not want humanity to know. If the devil can make Christians believe that the problem they have is just the flesh acting up or that Christians cannot be oppressed by the devil; then this lie will keep them from having blessings that God's Word is promising. When Christians know that it is satan coming to steal the Word of God out of their heart; and they know it IS NOT just their flesh or something other than a demon spirit, then the Christians of this world will have huge victories in their lives. They will know the truth and the truth will set them free!

The devil is our problem, not God, not the flesh, not the intellect!

Matthew 8:16: "...cast out devils..healed" (Notice: Get rid of source-demon-first).

Luke 4:40: "...all they that had any sick with divers diseases brought them unto Him; and He laid His hands on every one of them, and healed them. V.41. and devils also came *out of many*, crying...." (Note: The italicized phrase is the single Greek word, "polus". This Greek word is also rendered as: abundant, altogether, while, times). Clearly, demon spirits were present when sickness and diseases were present; and Jesus got to the root of the problems; He cast the demons out, and people were healed.

Matthew 8:16: "When the even was come, they brought unto Him many that were possessed with devils: and ***He cast out the spirits*** with His Word, AND HEALED all that were sick."

7

HOW TO SEE IN THE SPIRIT WORLD

In this chapter, I am going to give you Scriptures to show you how to see in the Spirit world and how to use the Gift of Discerning of Spirits that the Lord has already given us.

In Chapter 4, titled "Faith and Imagination," I talked a great deal about II Corinthians 4:17, 18. However, I want to look at it again from the perspective of instructions for seeing in the Spirit world.

Verse 17: "...a far more exceeding and eternal **weight** of glory. (Note: The italicized word, "weight" is the Greek word, "baros". This Greek word is also rendered as: a load of abundance, authority, profound, mystery, deepness). This Reputation of God for us today supersedes greatly that of what the Old Testament people were able to experience.

And then verse 18 explains how the Gift of Discerning of Spirits comes into operation: "***While we look*** not at the things which are seen, but at the things which are not seen: for the things which are seen are temporal, but the things which are not seen are eternal."

The Gift of Discerning of Spirits, the ability to see into the Spirit world comes into operation when ***we initiate*** our minds and spirits to see. Literally, we imagine we see in the Spirit world.

Keep in mind the italicized phrase, "*While we look*" is the Greek word, "skopeo". This Greek word is comparable to the Greek word, "optanomai". This Greek word is also rendered as: *mentally seeing or mentally having a vision*.

It is not as the Holy Spirit looks, but while we look. If we do not do it, it will not happen.

Keep in mind, that Jesus prayed that we would have the Reputation of God. He prayed that we would have the same glory that He had. If Jesus were in the presence of any human being right now, He could simply look into any human being's body and see if they had a demon spirit that was causing a problem in their body. So now we can, because Jesus always got His prayers answered.

John 14:12-14, tells us plainly that we can do the works of Jesus and greater.

At anytime Jesus could look at a person and see if there was a spirit of infirmity inside their body. So according to this verse, we can too.

Philippians 2:5: "God is giving us the invitation to have the mind of Christ. The decision is ours. If we accept this passage as truth, along with the many other Scriptures I've given in this book, then we can use our minds the same way Jesus did. At any time that thought entered into Jesus' mind to look supernaturally into someone's body to see if there was a demon spirit causing a problem; He could. And now we can. We need to imagine we have the mind of Christ.

I Corinthians 6:17, teaches us plainly that any person that is joined unto the Lord is one Spirit. If Jesus Christ is the Lord of our life, then we are one with Christ. If we are one with Christ, then we can do anything He did. My right eye is as much one with me as my left eye, and my right eye can do anything my left eye can do.

Ordination of Imagination

I Timothy 4:15: "*Meditate* upon these things; give thyself wholly *to them; that thy profiting* may appear to all." (Note: The italicized word, "Meditate" is the Greek word, "meletao". This Greek word is also translated as: *imagine*, revolve in the mind. Also the italicize phrase, "to them; that thy profiting" is the Greek word, "prokope". This Greek word is also translated as: progress, *advancement,* furtherance, increase).

Clearly, God has ordained us to use our imagination.

Accurately, this verse is translated: "Imagine upon God's Word; give thyself wholly to them; that thy advancement would appear to ALL!" This verse clearly validates that imagining God's Word is truth, brings healing, miracles and financial prosperity from the Divine Spirit world into the natural world.

First imagine, then it materializes. A phone call with Sid Roth, Wednesday, was very interesting: Sid said, he personally talked with a person that had information from a professional person that had studied the human mind. And Sid said, they found out recently that if a person imagines something, *__their physical body actually experiences the imagination__*. This also gives more validity to my teaching. Later on, Sid Roth, he had a program in which this subject was talked about in more detail with more validity.

Proverbs 23:7; "For as he thinketh in his heart, so is he...." (Note: The Bible clearly said, "thinking" and not "thought"). Thinking is imagining. God is saying again clearly, if we will imagine God's Word as truth it will materialize in this natural world.

As you study this passage, as well as the whole Bible, you find that quite often when the word "heart" is used it is in reference to a person's "spirit." Before any knowledge can get into a person's spirit, they must spend a lot of time putting this knowledge in their mind. This is a strong reason why I strongly encourage people to memorize the Word of God. It makes it easier to get the Word from one's mind into their spirit, if they memorize the Word of God.

Yes, imagination causes a natural appearance.

Initiating an Oracle

The Hebrew word for, "oracle" is, "dabar". A fuller meaning for the word, "dabar" is: a powerful word, "command" or "promises directly from God." The Greek word for, "oracle" is, "logion". The fuller meaning of the Greek word, "logion" is: "An utterance of God, a Divine Expression concerning doctrine."

Acts 7:36-38, gives us a good example of an oracle of God being manifested. This passage tells us the story of Moses on Mount Sinai when God spoke directly to him and gave him the Ten Commandments.

An oracle is the highest mandate, the highest command, the highest Supernatural order directly from God.

Another good example would be in Genesis 1:1-3: "In the beginning God created the heaven and the earth. V.2. And the earth was without form and void: and darkness was upon the face of the deep, and the Spirit of God moved upon the face of the waters. V.3. AND GOD SAID, LET THERE BE LIGHT: AND THERE WAS LIGHT."

Proverbs 29:18: "Where there is no *vision*, the people

perish: *but he that keepeth* the law, happy *is he."*

Notice that God used the words "vision" and "law" interchangeable. Why didn't God say, "Where there is no vision, the people perish: but he that keepeth the vision happy is he?"

The reason is, in the mind of God, if we are truly keeping His Word, we are visualizing, imagining God's Word as truth.

Let's interrogate this verse using a couple of the Hebrew words to get a clearer understanding and read of a PROFOUND REVELATION that is life changing for those who will believe God's Word.

The word, *"vision"* in this passage is the Hebrew word, "chazon". This Hebrew word is pronounced, "khaw-zone". The fuller meaning of this word is: *a sight, (mentally), that is, a dream, revelation, or ORACLE: vision, to gaze at; mentally to perceive, contemplate (with pleasure); specially to have a vision of: behold, look, prophesy, provide, see.*

Notice in Proverbs 29:18 the word, *"law"* is the Hebrew word, "tôrâh", which is clearly rendered throughout the Scriptures in reference to *God's commands or God's Word.*

Also notice the italicized phrase, *"but he that keepeth".* This phrase is the Hebrew word, "shamar". This Hebrew word can be translated into approximately 25 different words. All of these words are in reference to the word "keepeth". However, of the 25 words, there is also the word, "man". The word, "man" should be translated as, "they". By reading the full meaning of this word, as well as reading the rest of the Bible, this phrase accurately is translated as, *"but they that keepeth".* Also, the last italicized phrase, "is he", is not in the Hebrew whatsoever. Translators added this phrase in the hope that it would give a clearer meaning to this verse. However, a more accurate phrase would be, "are they".

61

Let's read Proverbs 29:18, and put the Hebrew full meaning in the place of vision and law: "Where there is no *mental dream, which is a revelation or an ORACLE,* the people perish: but *they* that keepeth God's commands, happy *are they*."

Looking at the full meaning of what God's Word is saying in Proverbs 29:18, we can clearly understand that if we take God's Word and purposely initiate seeing it as truth with our minds, we are having an Oracle of God!

Look again at the fuller meaning of the word, "vision" and the word, "law"; and you can clearly understand that God is clearly telling us that we can provide, with pleasure, a mental dream, and by doing this we are having the Highest Order of a powerful word or command directly from God.

God has ordained that we can have a vision, and oracle. The decision is ours.

So many people live and die waiting for God to give them an oracle; and God has been waiting on them to have as many as they like.

Keep in mind, "When an oracle of God is in manifestation, there isn't anything that will stop it"!

Fullfilleth All and All

Ephesians 1:22: "And hath put all things under His feet, and gave him to be the head over all things to the Church. V.23. Which is His body, *the fullness of Him that filleth* all in all." (Note: The italicized phrase in verse 23, "the fullness" is the Greek word, "pleroma". This Greek word is also translated as: *performance, fulfilling.)*

And the underlined italicized phrase, "of Him that filleth" is the Greek word, "pleroo". This Greek word is also

62

translated as: satisfy, *execute (an office), finish (a period or task), complete*, make full, fully preach, supply.

By looking at the fuller meaning of these words in verse 22, let's read this verse more accurately and more simply: "And God hath put all things under Jesus' feet, and God gave Jesus the position to be head over all things, and Jesus gave this authority to the Church. V.23. Which is His body, which fulfills His office on earth."

(Note: If we born again, Spirit-filled Christians are fulfilling completely the Office of Jesus, then we can see in the Spirit world anytime we so choose. Of course, that the Father be Glorified in the Son. John 14:12-14).

How I Use the Gift of Discerning of Spirits in Detail

Based upon the many Scriptures in this book; let me explain to you what I do, so you can do it also, that God would be glorified and that people would be blessed.

If the Office of Discerning of Spirits (Office of a Prophet) is not in manifestation; I choose to operate in the Supernatural to give God glory and to bless people. So, I look at people and then I close my eyes so I can focus more in the Spirit world. Regardless if the person is red, yellow, black or white; I see a silhouette of that person (I am convinced that there is only one race; which is the human race. And we are all the same color in the Spirit, which I see as clear). Then I look for dark images. The Bible clearly gives us many Scriptures which validates satan's kingdom being the kingdom of darkness. Scriptures such as Ephesians 6:12: "For we wrestle not against flesh and blood, but against principalities, against powers, against the ***rulers of the darkness*** of the

63

world, against spiritual wickedness in high places."

When I find the dark image, I command it to leave in the Name of Jesus. I initiate seeing the image (the demon spirit) leaving. Then I initiate, with my imagination seeing God's Glory (in sunlight splendor, which is the hiding place of His power, Habakkuk 3:4). (Notice the Amplified Bible as it is absolutely correct in the Hebrew for Habakkuk 3:4.) I see the sunlight splendor going from my hand into the area of their body creating health or recreation.

I then instruct the people to focus on relief, relaxing based upon Romans 6:19, where the Bible teaches us that as we have yielded to unrighteousness, so now yield to righteousness unto holiness. (Note: In Romans 6:19, the Greek word for, "righteousness" is, "dikaiosune"). This Greek word is also translated as: justification, innocent. And the Greek word for, "holiness" is, "hagisamost". This Greek word is translated as: purification, purity, blameless. God is much, much more powerful than satan; holiness is much, much more powerful than unholiness; so it is easier to yield to holiness than it is to yield to sin.

The word, "yield" in most dictionaries will give a co-equal term as, "to surrender" and, "surrender" has the same meaning as, "relax". Most people understand the term, "relax" when receiving God's Anointing, rather than using the word, "yield". We find throughout the Scriptures of God's great power working as people would yield or surrender, which is relaxing and letting God's power come into their life and presence. Let's look at a couple of verses that help validate this doctrine:

Exodus 14:13: "And Moses said unto the people, Fear *ye not, stand* still and see the salvation of the Lord, which He will shew to you today...." (Note: The italicized phrase is the Hebrew word, "yatsab". This Hebrew word is also translated as: reflex; and one of the meanings of, "reflex" is, "to relax," which is the opposite of, "flex"). We also understand the word, "still" also co-equally means to, "be restful, to become motionless," and that is what a person does when they relax.

Notice what happened when God's people simply stood still, when they relaxed. They saw, they experienced the miracle working power of God; they saw the Red Sea that was about 1,700 feet deep separate and they walked through the midst of the sea on dry ground.

Relaxing is giving up our ability and surrendering to God's ability. Look at Psalm 46:10: "*Be still*, and know that I am God: I will be exalted among the heathen, I will be exalted in the earth."

Notice the italicized phrase, "Be still", which is the Hebrew word, "raphah". This Hebrew word is also translated as: faint, be feeble, idle, be weak. All of the words that are co-equal terms for the phrase, "Be still" have the exact same meaning as, "relax".

God is letting us know that there is a time when we simply need to relax and trust totally on Him.

Ephesians 6:13,14: "Wherefore take unto you the whole armor of God, that ye may be able to withstand in the evil day, and having done all, to *stand*. V.14. *STAND* ...."

Notice the italicized word, "stand" in this passage. The Greek word for the word, "stand" is, "histemi". This word is also with the same meaning as: lay, horizontal posture, reflexive and utterly prostrate, lay down.

So, we must do everything that we can do, spiritually, mentally and physically and then just relax and let God do His part and we then will experience God's miracle working power.

Relaxing is Conceiving

Mark 11:24: "Therefore I say unto you, what things soever ye desire, when ye pray, believe that ye receive them, and ye shall have them."

Jesus clearly taught us that receiving comes before having. The Greek word for, "receive" in this passage is, "lambano", which is also translated as: accept. Most dictionaries will agree that receiving is something that is done in a relaxed state, it's not obtaining something that you earned. It's not something obtained by strenuous efforts at all.

So when we have the understanding in our mind and spirit that we are relaxing our spirits, minds and bodies, we are actually conceiving, receiving God's miracle seed, we will then have a miracle.

Next, I teach the people that I have just released God's miracle power into their body and they should focus on the relief and not the past problem. Jesus said in Matthew 7:7 and Luke 11:9: "...to seek and ye shall find." (Note: The Greek word for, "seek" is, "zeteo"). This Greek word is also translated as: *desire*, enquire, *to worship God* or *in a bad sense to plot against life*.

So, when we see, inquire, look for, search for pain or whatever we prayed to be rid of, what we are actually doing is desiring in a bad sense to plot against life.

However, if we seek, inquire, desire relief, that is exactly what we will get. Jesus said, "seek and you will find". You will get whatever you are looking for.

Actions Activate God's Power

James 2:19: "Thou believest that there is one God: thou

66

doest well: the devils also believe, and tremble. V.20. but wilt thou know, O vain man, that faith without **works** is dead?" (Note: The italicized word, "works" is the Greek word, "ergon". This Greek word is also translated as: to work, an effort, an act, doing, labor). So, if we say we believe God's Word, but have no actions that correspond with what we say, we are believing two things: No. 1. We have devil faith; as the devils of hell say they believe also, but you will never get the devils of hell to act kind or demonstrate God's love. They will not have corresponding actions of God's Word. No. 2. We have dead faith.

So I encourage people to take the final step of receiving their miracle, which is actions to the best of their ability.

How I Use the Gift of Discerning of Spirits in Simplicity

I look at a person. I close my eyes and see their silhouette. I look for dark images, knowing it is a demon spirit. I command the demon to leave. I command that area where the demon was to relax, understanding that relaxing is surrendering, accepting God's miracle power. I then tell the person to focus on relief, letting them know that demons will come back if they seek for them, so seek for relief. Then, I tell the person to do something they could not do before or something that was difficult to do in the past.

As I said previously, if the Office of Discerning of Spirits is not initiated by God, I then initiate the Gift of Discerning of Spirits. I've been doing this since at least 1977 and it is **extremely rare** if there isn't an instant manifestation of healing, relief, or a recreation of a bodily part. I cast the demons out in the Name of Jesus and command the areas of the person's body that needs a healing or a miracle to surrender, relax, and receive their miracle.

Understanding Demons

There are times that I see a demon spirit, and I ask the person if they have a problem there, and they say no. Sometimes they may say, I've never had a problem there.

I have confidence that God is smarter than me and smarter than the human race. Based upon so many Scriptures that I've given in this book, and based upon over 700 verses in my book, "Mystery of the Ages" I say this with great humility and great respect to God and His Word, if my imagination says I see a demon spirit then it is there regardless of what anyone or anything else says. I still cast the demon out.

We must understand that demons are not permanent entities; they can move around. They are also deceivers. They will sometimes move from one area of the body to another to try to deceive you, so you will leave them alone.

Another fact, is that the demon may have just arrived in that area of that person's body, and in the future they will have a problem.

Several years ago, I was in a service and while I was preaching I happened to look at a man and I noticed right under his left rib cage a demon spirit, and I heard the word, "spleen". At that time, I had no idea where a spleen was located. This was a time when the Office of Discerning of Spirits was in operation. However, I have had similar experiences with the Gift of Discerning of Spirits in which I initiated.

The man was dressed in a very nice expensive suit. Then I told him what I saw and the word that I heard. I asked him if I could pray for him. Very respectfully the man declined and then explained that he just had a checkup from his doctor, which was one of the best in the area. He also said that it was unusual that I mentioned his spleen since his doctor made mention of it for the first time in all the years that he has gone to this doctor for examinations. He said his doctor said, "I've never seen a spleen look so good"!

I asked the man if I could pray for him anyway, as it would not hurt anything. And three times he said, "No, my spleen is good, thank you anyway". Six months later the man's spleen exploded and he died.

Our motive must be to love and care for people. And we must never exalt any knowledge above the knowledge of God's Word. If God says we have His mind, we have it.

8

BENEFITS OF IMAGINATION

Again, when we are talking about the Gift of Discerning of Spirits, we are talking about using our imagination. We are imagining that God's Word is truth. We are mentally initiating the fact that we have the mind of Christ. We are initiating the fact that we can see in the Spirit as we will, just as Christ did and does.

I took about 30 minutes and found 240 verses in the Old Testament that talk about humans using their imagination, and 56 times in the New Testament. I can see that if a person wanted to, they could do a huge study just on the word, "imagination" in the Bible.

You will find many different words that have the Hebrew or Greek word meaning, "imagination", however many times it is not only translated, "imagination", but also see, sight, vision, mind, meditate.

So it is very evident that imagination is ordained of God and it is a very strong doctrine in the Bible.

Let's look at some of the benefits of using our imagination in agreement with God's Word. Imagining God's Word as truth!

Looking at the Old Testament

I only want to give a few references in the Old Testament to help validate the benefits of Scriptural Imagination.

One hundred and twenty one times the Hebrew word, "chashab" is used in the Old Testament.

This Hebrew word is translated as: *to plot from the mental effort, to think, regard, conceive, imagine, purpose, think,* to invent. Clearly, this Hebrew word is describing, "Imagination". This Hebrew word, "chashab", which also is rendered as, "imagination" is translated many times in the Old Testament as, "imagination".

Genesis 50:20: (uses the Hebrew word, "chashab") "But as for you, ye thought evil against me; but God *meant* it unto good...." (Note: God uses His imagination to cause good things to materialize from the Divine World into the natural world for us.

A Good Father Leads by Example!

Psalm 1:1: "*Blessed* is the man that walketh not in the counsel of the ungodly.... V.2. But his delight is in the law of the Lord; and in His law *doth he meditate* day and night." (Note: The italicized word, "Blessed" is the Hebrew word, "esher". The full meaning of the word is: happiness, prosperous). When we receive God's happiness and prosperity, it is Divine. Notice also the italicized phrase, "doth he meditate" is the Hebrew word, "hagah". Hagah is also translated as: ponder, *imagine*, study.

(Note: We become happy, financially prosperous by using our God given ability to imagine God's Word as truth. When we take God's Word and put it into our imagination

71

God word imagenation

life, we are actually experiencing the real world, the Divine World.)

Psalm 63:6: "When I remember thee upon my bed, *and mediate* on thee in the night watches. V.7. Because thou hast been *my help*...." (Note: The italicized phrase, "and mediate" is the Hebrew word, "hagah". Hagah's full meaning is: ponder, *imagine*, study. Also the italicized phrase, "my help" is the Hebrew word, "ezrah". Ezrah's full meaning is: aid, to surround, that is protect)

Psalm 77:12: "*I will meditate* also of all thy work, and talk of thy doings. V.14. Thou art the God that doest *wonders*...." (Note: The italicized phrase, "I will meditate" is the Hebrew word, "hagah". This Hebrew word is also translated as: *imagine*, study. Also the italicized word, "wonders" is the Hebrew word, "pele". This Hebrew word is also translated as: a miracle, marvelous thing).

David had a history of experiences where God did great wonders and marvelous miracles for him. According to Psalm 63:6, David would mediate upon those great miracles that God did for him.

I am sure he meditated upon those things to give him confidence for future miracles that he would need.

In like manner, if we continue to meditate on the great things God did for people in the Bible and the great things God has done in our lives, we too would have great confidence for miracles that we will need in the future. Another good practice is to imagine victories over problems you may have now. Use God's Word as the source for imagining the problem solved supernaturally. Proverbs 23:7: "As a person thinketh (imagines) in their heart, so are they!"

Isaiah 26:3: "Thou wilt keep *him in perfect peace, whose mind* is stayed on thee: because **he** *trusteth* in thee." (Note: The italicized phrase, "him in perfect peace" is the single Hebrew word, "shalom". Shalom is also translated as: safety, well, happy, welfare, health, prosperity, favor, perfect, rest, wholly. The word, "him" is not within this Hebrew word, neither are there any words within this word that could possibly be in reference to the word, "him". Also the italicized phrase, "*he trusteh*" is the single Hebrew word, "batach". Batach is also translated as: confident or *sure, be bold, secure, woman, hope* and the word, "he" is not within this Hebrew word at all, neither is there any words within this word that could possibly be in reference to the word, "he"). Also, the underlined italicized phrase "*whose mind*" is the Hebrew word, "yetser". Yetser is also translated as: *imagination*, word.

You can actually sum up this verse as saying it's meaning is being, "blessed in every area of life and Godliness". And this Divine Blessing comes from us initiating imagination of God's Word!

Jeremiah 29:11: "For I know *the thoughts that I think* toward you, saith the Lord, **thoughts of peace** and not of evil, to give *you an expected end.*" (Note: The italicized phrase, "the thoughts" and the italicized word, "thoughts", is the Hebrew word, "machashabah", which is also translated as: *imagination*. Also the underlined italicized phrase, "that I think" is the Hebrew word, "chashab", which is also translated as: *imagine.* Also the italicized word, "peace" is the Hebrew word, "shalom" being co-equally translated as: *safe, happy*, **health, prosperity, perfect, wholly.** Also the italicized phrase, "you an expected" is the Hebrew word, "tiqvah", which is also translated as: *hope, expectancy.* And the last italicized word "end" is the Hebrew word, "achariyth", which is also translated as: *future.*

Let's look at this verse with the fuller meaning from the Hebrew, as well as from the foundation of the Holy Scriptures: "For I God, know my imaginations I have toward you, saith the Lord, imaginations and intentions of safety, financial prosperity, health, perfection, happiness, wholeness and completeness in your body, and not of evil in the least, and to give you divine hope, and wonderful expectation for your future."

Again, God uses His imagination to create a wonderful life for every single human being. You are extremely valuable and precious to God.

In the Old Testament the Hebrew word, "nephesh" is written 672 times. This word is also translated as: mental desire, pleasure. Let's look at a couple of verses that uses this Hebrew word. Proverbs 19:15: "Slothfulness casteth into a deep sleep; and an idle *soul* shall suffer hunger." (Note: The italicized word, "soul" is the Hebrew word, "nephesh").

God is letting us know that our imagination can feed our stomachs. I've built houses and I would imagine my work for the next day while lying in bed. Then the next day, it was easy to do the work, it was as if I had done it before. And I did, in my imagination. We need to use our imagination for our needs being meet.

Psalm 23:3: "He restoreth my *soul*:" The italicized word, "soul" is the Hebrew word, "nephesh". (Note: God restores our imagination, He wants it to be new every morning, Lamentations 3:22, 23).

Looking at the New Testament

Optanomai

Optanomai is a Greek word that is used 56 times in the

New Testament. Optanomai is translated as: to gaze, *to discern clearly mentally*; to experience perceiving, *seeing*. By reading these words that describe the word, "optanomai" we can understand clearly this word is talking about, "imaginations".

If a person is discerning and seeing mentally, they most definitely are using their imagination.

Optanomai is used strongly in the New Testament in reference to manifesting God's Greatest Blessings in the natural world. Optanomai is a Supernatural source, power that brings things out of the Divine Spirit World into the natural world; to glorify God and to bless humanity.

Let's look at a few verses in the New Testament that uses the word, "optanomai". (Note: Each time I *italicized* a word or a phrase; understand that it is the Greek word, "optanomai" that is being used).

Matthew 5:8: "Blessed are the pure in heart: for they shall *see* God." (Note: Keep in mind, that the Father, Son and the Holy Ghost are 3 persons but ONE God. Just as water has 3 manifestations, water, ice and vapor. However, all of them are water). This passage verifies John 14:21 where Jesus said, "He that hath my commandments, *and keepeth* them, he it is that loveth me: and he that loveth me shall be loved of my Father, and I will love *him, and will manifest* myself to him. (Notice the italicized phrase, "and keepeth" is the Greek word, "tereo". Optanomai is a root word for this Greek word; so again, Jesus is talking about imagining God's Word. Also notice the italicized phrase, "him, and "will manifest" which is the Greek word, "emphanizo". This Greek word is also translated as: to exhibit in person, to appear.

Clearly, Jesus is telling us how we can get confidence, faith in Jesus appearing to us! (Note: This is how strong and

75

valid imagination is. It puts us in a place where we can see Jesus face to face in the natural).

Matthew 17:3: "And behold, there *appeared* unto them Moses and Elias talking with him." (Note: This is what Jesus did and this is how He was supernaturally strengthened)!

Luke 1:11: "*And there appeared* unto him an angel of the Lord standing on the right side of the altar of incense an angel of the Lord appeared to Zacharias."

Luke 22:43: "*And there appeared* an angel unto him from heaven, strengthening him."

Luke 24:34 saying: "The Lord is risen indeed, *and hath appeared* to Simon."

John 11:40: "Jesus saith unto her, Said I not unto thee, that if thou wouldest believe, *thou shouldest see* the glory of God?"

John 11:41: "Then they took away the stone from the place where the dead was laid. And Jesus lifted *up his eyes*, and said, Father, I thank thee that thou hast heard me." (Note: The italicized phrase, "up his eyes" is the Greek word, "opthalmos". This Greek word is translated also as, "vision" and its root word is, "optanomai").

Jesus raised Lazarus from the dead by using His imagination. I've raised the dead corpse and that is exactly what I do, I see with my mind's eye, with my imagination the person alive, "and they come alive".

Acts 7:2: "And he said, Men, brethren, and fathers, hearken: The God of glory *appeared* unto our father Abraham...."

Acts 9:17: "And Ananias went his way, and entered into the house; and putting his hands on him said, Brother Saul, the Lord, even Jesus, *that appeared* unto thee in the way as thou camest, hath sent me, that thou mightest receive they sight, and be filled with the Holy Ghost." (Note: The word, "optanomai" can be translated co-equally as, "to gaze with wide open eyes, as at something remarkable," as well as, "to discern clearly, to see mentally").

So, we are not positive which kind of vision that the Apostle Paul had, as the Greek word can be used both ways. Regardless, it lets us know how powerful imagination is; as it is taken from the same Greek word exactly in reference to seeing something remarkable with the eyes wide open (a supernatural encounter).

And we know, as we study the book of Acts and the Epistles, how this supernatural experience changed Paul's life. As well as, the multi-millions of people's lives have been changed because of such an experience and many more.

Acts 16:9: "And a vision *appeared* to Paul in the night; There stood a man of Macedonia, and prayed him saying...."

Acts 26:16: "But rise, and stand upon thy feet: *for I have appeared* unto thee for this purpose, to make thee a minister and a witness both of these things which thou hast seen, and of those things in which *I will appear* unto thee;" (Note: Jesus said, "he appeared and Jesus ordained that he would appear). Keep in mind, this is the word that co-equally is rendered for imagination. We know that Jesus was talking about imaginations, as well as a natural vision, because He operated both; with imaginations and natural visions. We can say the same thing about the Apostle Paul. Also, the Word of God endorses that humanity have both kinds of visions, those of the natural and of the imagination. (Note: An initiated imagination is as powerful as a vision initiated by God - as an angel appearing to you or as Jesus appearing to you).

I Corinthians 15:5: "*And that he was seen* of Cephas, then of the twelve:"

I Corinthians 15:7: "After *that, he was seen* of James; then of all the apostles."

I Corinthians 15:8: "And last of all *he was seen* of me

also, as of one born out of due time."

Hebrews 12:14: "Follow peace with all men, and holiness, without which no man **shall see** theLord:" (Note: Peace and Holiness in our lives plays a huge part of having visions and for our imaginations to be manifested by God).

9

WHAT ABOUT ERROR?

In this chapter, I want to give us some Scriptures that will prevent us from getting into error. Everything that God has is pure and holy. However, the devil likes to counterfeit everything that God does. The Bible teaches us especially in the Last Days how satan will have false Signs & Wonders. However, there has to be the real thing before satan can come up with a counterfeit.

Let's examine some famous passages in the Bible that the devil has used to keep Christians from allowing God's Supernatural to take place in their lives.

One of the famous passages that the devil uses to keep Christians from allowing God's Supernatural to flow through them is Matthew 7:22: "MANY WILL SAY TO ME IN THAT DAY, Lord, Lord, have we not prophesied in thy name? And in thy name have cast out devils? And in thy name done many wonderful works? V.23. ***And then will I profess unto them, I never knew you***: depart from me, ye that work iniquity." This passage has been used by the devil so strongly to frighten people from allowing the Supernatural Gifts and Callings of the Holy Spirit to flow from them. However, simply by reading the passage you can see the truth that separates satan's false from God's will.

They Were Not Christians

Verse 23 is the key in understanding verse 22. Clearly, this group of people are not Christians and never accepted Jesus as their Lord. Of course, they will lie to try to keep from going to hell. They are liars, just as they called Him Lord, and He is not their Lord, because Jesus said, "I NEVER knew you!" So shall they lie about casting out devils and doing wonderful works. Sinners always lie; how much more will they lie to try to keep from going to hell; thinking by lying they can avoid going to hell.

MAt. 7:22 In verse 24, Jesus gives the comfort of knowing how to avoid being a lying non-Christian: "Therefore whosoever heareth these sayings of mine, and doeth them, I will liken him unto a wise man, which built his house upon a rock."

Sign Seekers

Matthew:16:4: "A wicked and adulterous generation seeketh after a sign; and there shall no sign be given unto it, but the sign of the prophet Jonas."

No. 1. We are not seeking signs, they simply follow the believer (Mark 16:17).

No. 2. We are not wicked and adulterous. We are Holy people of God. We do not smoke, drink, curse, watch evil movies, gossip, etc.

No. 3. Healings, miracles, casting out devils, raising the dead will not be good enough for this group, they want something apart from the Scriptures, something different than what Jesus did. This group are very much aware of the Signs & Wonders Jesus did, but they do not want that, they want something that is not Scriptural. However, true believers follow the Word of God and follow the mandates of God's Word. For we are to do what Jesus did (John 14:12-14).

False Christ's

Matthew 24:24: "For there shall arise false Christs, and false prophets, and shall show great signs and wonders; insomuch that, if *it were possible*, they shall deceive the very elect."

No. 1. We do not say we are Christ (There is only one!) A true child of God that allows God's supernatural to flow through them, is extremely humble, and they give all the Glory to the Lord; they know it is God's grace and God's power that is working through them. They fully understand that they are only a vessel that God uses for His Glory and His honor.

No. 2. The passage also says about these false workers of false signs and wonders, "IF it were possible, they shall deceive the very elect". However, it is not possible, the very elect are strongly founded in God's Word and they will not be deceived. You never have to worry about getting into error if you have plenty of good, sound, clear Scripture to validate your beliefs.

Lying Signs & Wonders

II Thessalonians 2:9: "Even him, whose coming is after the working of satan *with all* power and signs *and lying* wonders. V.10. And with all deceivableness *of unrighteousness*; in them that perish; because they received not the love of the truth, that they might be saved."

81

(Let's analyze this passage to get to the truth of what is being said. No.1. This is talking about the antichrist, and so these things will also be manifested among antichrist people. No. 2. This passage has nothing to do with those who love the Lord, those who promote God's Word above everything else. Knowing you cannot separate Christ from the Word of God, people that love God's Word and promote it above everything else are not in the least antichrist (anti-Bible).

Notice the first italicized phrase, "*with all*"; this is the Greek word, "pas". This Greek word is also translated as: *Including all the forms of declension or moral deterioration, worsened kind of state, falling off or away, an enfeebled and worsened kind of state.* Also notice the second italicized phrase, "*and lying*"; this is the Greek word, "pseudos", and is also translated as: *falsehood, to utter an untruth or attempt to deceive by falsehood, wrongfulness, unjust, unrighteousness, and wicked, by implication treacherous, specifically heathen.*

Notice verse 10. The first italicized phrase is the Greek word, "adikia" which is also translated as: *wrongfulness, unjust, wicked, by implication treacherous.*

Also notice in verse 10, it is plainly written who these people are: "them that perish; because they received not the love of the truth, that they might be saved."

Revelation 13:13: "And he doeth great wonders, so that he maketh fire come down from heaven on the earth in the sight of men."

This is talking about the false prophet during the 7 year tribulation period.

Notice again, he is doing lying signs and wonders and trying to get people's attention to follow him by doing things that Jesus did not do.

Note: We are not making fire come down from Heaven!

We are healing the sick, casting out devils, raising the dead; doing the works of Jesus (John 14:12-14).

Casting Down Wrong

II Corinthians 10:5: "Casting down imaginations, and every high thing that exalteth itself against the knowledge of God, and bringing into captivity every thought to the obedience of Christ...."

(Note: We must cast down imaginations that do not agree with God's Word, and keep and nurture the ones that do. Imagination is part of faith, so we *imagine in agreement with God's Word.*)

Refusing Condemnation

Intro: Understanding a demon spirit of condemnation.

When you start to allow this Gift of Discerning of Spirits to flow from you, understand satan is not going to like it. When you start allowing all of the Gifts of the Holy Spirit to flow through you, satan is not going to like it at all. In fact, the more you do for God, you can rest assured the devil is going to get real mad. Please understand two things. No. 1. It's a good sign that you do great things for God. So this is a good confirmation that you are in the will of God. No. 2. KNOW that: "Greater is He that is in you, than he that is in the world" (I John 4:4). So do not fear or be concerned, as when the devil and his demons start coming against you; this is a good opportunity for great promotion in your life. James 1:2: God says, ..."to count it all joy when you have temptations;" (the Greek word for "temptations" is, "peirasmos", this word is also translated as: adversity, trial or test).

Then the Lord tells us why we should count it all joy in verse 4, "that we may be perfect and entire wanting nothing." If we will be patient and trust the Lord during adversities, test, trails and temptations; what was meant for evil, God will turn for our good. Trials, test, temptation, adversities are the battle ground that allows us to be, "perfect, entire and wanting nothing". You could say it this way, "Big Battles, Produce Bigger Victories"!

In Mark, Chapter 4, Jesus said, "Where the Word is sown; satan comes immediately, to try to steal the Word. The Word of God destroys satan's kingdom, and part of his kingdom is doctrine of man, which is the same thing as doctrines of devils.

The devil will use people that profess to be Christians to try to intimidate and stop you. It was religious people that were so full of hate that hung Jesus on the cross. Keep in mind, that doctrines of devils is under the category of religion. Occults, cults are religions.

We must continue to walk in love toward those people and do not stoop down to their level and get in strife with them. Strife will blind your eyes to the point you will not be able to see and operate with God's blessings. God does not do this. It is the devil that blinds the eyes of people that get into sin (II Corinthians Chapter 4). It's like someone giving you a luxurious brand new car. You have the title, the keys, it's yours. You understand how to drive it, how to use all of the options in the car. But if you go blind, you will not be able to use it. You still have the understanding of how to drive it, but if you do, you will have a wreck and possibly kill yourself or someone else.

God never takes His blessings from us; however, if we get into sin, our eyes will be blinded and we cannot enjoy what God has given us.

"For there are certain men crept in unawares, who were before of old ordained to this ___condemnation, ungodly men, turning___ the grace of our God into lasciviousness, and denying the only Lord God and our Lord Jesus Christ." (Note: The italicized word, "condemnation" is the Greek word, "krima" and this Greek word's fuller meaning is: ___damnation, judgment, go to sue at the law, punish).___

The italicized word, "ungodly" is the Greek word, "asebes" and its fuller meaning is: ___negative, irreverent, wicked, impious.___

Also notice, the underlined italicized phrase, "men turning" is the Greek word, "metatithem" and this Greek word's fuller meaning is: transfer, exchange, ___pervert, remove___. The word, "men" is not in this Greek word at all, neither are there any words within this word that could be possibly in reference to the word, "men"; so people would be the accurate translation in place of the word, "men".

Notice this, that anyone who continually damns and condemns people, clearly the Bible says, "they are ungodly people", not Godly. They are not saved. They are in doctrines of devils. These type of people are negative and are extremely irreverent and they will take you to court if they can.

Love them, and stay away from them. Do not let their demonic influence spoil the love of God in your life.

These people may say this verse does not apply to them. However, if they are a condemner, a judger, a damner, this verse applies to them. They are denying the Word of God, which is denying the Lord Jesus Christ (because Jesus is the Word of God — John 1:1;14 and Revelation 19:13).

In great depths of the love of God, let me give the clear, accurate, full meaning of Jude verse 4: "*For there are certain people crept in unawares, who were before of old ordained, they are strongly under satan's influence to condemn, damn, punish people, they are ungodly wicked people."*

These type of people are very jealous people and do not have a ministry. The devil uses an ancient old demonic deceptive trick with them. He tells them, if they tear down others that are doing great things, this will cause the people that listen to these ungodly people to think, "wow", this ungodly person is smarter and more talented than anyone else; so I need to follow them and forsake all others.

In great, great depths of love, again, please let me encourage you not to be offended, and let me encourage you to not pay any attention to them and avoid them. And most of all, do not condemn them.

The Foundation of the Bible

The foundation of the whole Bible is John 3:16: "For God so love the world, that He gave His only begotten Son, that whosoever believeth in Him should not perish, but have everlasting life."

However, in the original writings of the Bible, there are no punctuation marks, no chapters or verses in the original writings. So verse 17 is part of verse 16 and is co-equally as important. Most people that have gone to Church only a few times know John 3:16, however, most people that know the Bible very well do not know John 3:17: "For ***God sent not His Son into the world not to condemn*** the world; but that the world through Him might be saved."

John 3:16, 17, is the foundation of the whole Bible. God is not a condemner and we that are true Christians are not either. So be real cautious that you do not condemn the condemner.

A Form of Godliness

In this little subtopic, I want to address the root of a problem of religious people (people bound by doctrines of man). Please make sure that you use this information in this little short subtopic to:

No. 1. Understand the source of this demonic spirit of criticism is from satan's kingdom through religious people to stop God's Last Day's Signs and Wonders. The devil knows if he can stop the Last Day's Signs and Wonders of God, he then can stop the Rapture from taking place. The Last Day's Signs and Wonders is one of the most important events that God wants accomplished before He can allow the Rapture to take place. And if the devil can stop it, he then stops the Rapture from taking place. The devil knows that he will be cast into the lake of fire in the Last Days and he wants to stop this from happening. I talk more about this subject in my book, "Neglecting the Ministry of Signs and Wonders is Neglecting the Rapture".

No. 2. We must MAKE SURE that we do not get in strife with condemning people. II Timothy 2:24: "And the servant of the Lord, ***MUST NOT STRIVE***, but be gentle unto all men...." (Note: Stife is sin, and sin blinds our eyes and deafens our ears, where we cannot see or hear God's blessings that He has already given us).

87

Separate, Depart

I've dealt with the issue in extreme measures personally, and I've counseled with many people along the lines of staying in a Church setting that has only a form of Godliness and no power thereof. People think God has put them in that Church setting (or denomination) to help those people see the light that we have. However, their organization is set up by the law to go by their man-made doctrines. So when you go against it, you are actually breaking the law.

Secondly, God tells us, "to come out from among them". You will not turn them around. You will only cause horrible problems for yourself and many others.

Let's read what God has to say about this situation.

II Timothy 3:1: "This know also, that in the Last Days perilous times shall come. V.2. For men shall be lovers of their ownselves, covetous, boasters, proud, blasphemers, disobedient to parent, unthankful, unholy, V.3. Without natural affection, trucebreakers, false accusers, incontinent, fierce, despisers of those that are good, V.4. Traitors, heady, highminded, lovers of pleasures more than lovers of God; V.5. Having a form of godliness, but denying *the power* thereof: from such *turn away*." (Note: The italicized phrase, "*the power*" is the Greek word, "doo-nam-is". This Greek words, fuller meaning is: specifically miraculous power, usually by implication, a miracle itself, worker of miracles, mighty wonderful works. Also the italicized phrase, "turn away" is the Greek word, "apotrepo". This Greek word is also translated as: deflect, avoid, separation, departure.

You may not see all of the things happening in that Church, ministry or denomination as spelled out in II Timothy 3:1-4. However, verse 5 will be very obvious - there is NO demonstration of the miracle working power of God;.

the Gifts and Offices of the Holy Spirit are not in operation there. The Apostle Paul said in I Corinthians 2:4: "That his speech and preaching was not with enticing words of man's wisdom; BUT WAS WITH DEMONSTRATION OF THE SPIRIT AND POWER." (Note: The word, "Power" in verse 5 is the same Greek word, "Power" in II Timothy 3:5).

The Lord was very kind and gentle with me many years ago; but He did tell me that I only had 1/2 of a ministry if the Gifts of the Holy Spirit and the Miracle Working Power of God was not in each service. The Lord told me to look at Mark 16:20, where the Lord worked with the people in ministry and CONFIRMED HIS WORD WITH SIGNS FOLLOWING. (Note: The word, "confirmed" in this verse has a great definition in the Webster's Dictionary which is: Establish the truth, accurately, with validity, or genuineness, confirm suspicions, ***to make valid or binding legally, to establish the truth, accuracy, validity, or genuineness of; verify, prove, substantiate, authenticate).***

Also notice the word, "signs", which is the Greek word, "semeion", this Greek word is also translated as, "the supernatural miracles in the senses realm confirming the atoning work of Christ."

More accurately, you could say a true Church has the Word of God taught and preached and then the ***Holy Spirit is allowed to confirm His Word with Signs following***.

There may be some things going on, but if there is no confirmation of the Word of God with Signs following in each service, really it's not a Church. It may be a form of a Church, but it is not a Church; and God said, "to come out from among them".

Romans 16:17: "Now I beseech you, brethren, mark them which cause divisions and offences contrary to the doctrine which ye have learned: and avoid them. V.18. For

89

they that are such serve not our Lord Jesus Christ, but their own belly; and by good words and fair speeches deceive the hearts of the simple."

Beware of Wolves

Matthew 7:15,16: "Beware of false prophets, which come to you in sheep's clothing, but inwardly they are ravening wolves. V.16. Ye shall know *them by their fruits* ..." (Note: The italicized phrase, "them by their fruits" is the exact same word, "fruits" appearing in Galatians 5:22, where the fruits of the Holy Spirit are explained as: God's unconditional love, peace, longsuffering, gentleness, goodness, faith, meekness, temperance).

10

GOD'S GRACE

The purpose of this chapter is to give you confidence that you qualify for the Gift of Discerning of Spirits to operate in your life if Jesus is the Lord of your life (you've been born again) and if you are filled with the Holy Spirit with the evidence of speaking in tongues.

Actually, this Gift has already been given to the whole human race, but if people are not born again they cannot see the Gift. They do not understand the Gift at all. I Corinthians 2:14 teaches us plainly, "But the natural man received not the things of the Spirit of God: for they are foolishness unto him: neither can he know them, because they are spiritually discerned."

If a person has not been born again, they have a dead spirit and cannot hear God's voice very well. They understand very little the things of God. God loves every single human being equally, and He has made sure that every human has a certain amount of faith, trust, confidence that there is a God and He wants to give them Divine life. Romans 12:3 gives us some understanding along these lines: "....according as God hath dealt to every *man the measure* of faith." (Note: The italicized phrase is the single Greek word, "met'ron"). This Greek word has the fuller meaning of: a limited portion or degree. The word, "man" is not within the meaning of this word at all, neither are there any words within this word that could possibly be in reference to the word "man". Accurately, this phrase would be translated, "person the measure".

When a person has not been filled with the Holy Spirit with the evidence of speaking in tongues, they can only have an Old Testament experience, which is extremely shallow, and may not happen in their entire life, because of not being sensitive to the Holy Spirit. When a person has been filled with the Holy Spirit, they are more sensitive to the Holy Spirit as now He lives in them 24 hours per day.

Let's look at the Grace of God in some verses to give you confidence to flow with the Gift of Discerning of Spirits which is the ability to see in the Spirit world.

God Ordained Imagination for Humanity From the Beginning

I went into detail about Genesis 11:6 in Chapter 4. So read the information again with the understanding that these people were not born again, they were non-reverencing people toward God. They were heathens. However, the Supernatural power of Imagination would have worked for them, because this verse says, "And the Lord said: "...NOTHING will be restrained from them which they have imagined to do." In the very next verse God said He was going to have to stop them by confounding their language. My point here is the clear fact that the Supernatural power of God in the imagination realm could work for ungodly people, people that were not born again. SO HOW MUCH MORE WILL IT WORK FOR YOU!!! And of course, if you are born again and filled with the Holy Spirit, the accuracy, the fluency will be EXTREMELY compounded. As we have a new covenant established upon better promises (Hebrews 6:9; 7:19; 22; 8:6; John 17:22), where Jesus prayed that we that shall believe would have the same Glory (the same Reputation) that He had. Keep in mind, that Jesus always got His prayers answered!

God

Romans teaches us that ungodly people know about the invisible things of God. It teaches they know about the Supernatural power of imagination.

Let's read and analyze Romans 1:18-20: "***For the wrath*** of God is revealed from heaven against all ungodliness and unrighteousness of men, who hold the truth in unrighteousness; V.19. Because that which may be known of God is manifest in them; for God hath showed it unto them. V.20. For the invisible things of Him from the creation of the world are clearly seen, being understood by the things that are made, even His eternal power and Godhead; so that they are without excuse:" (Note: There is so much to be analyzed so we can see some deep truths of God with simplicity. So, first of all, let's look at the first italicized phrase, "for the wrath". This phrase is the single Greek word, "orge". The fuller meaning of this word is: properly desire (as a reaching forth, passion. I realize that this word can be used as wrath also; however, when interpreting Scripture a person has to make sure: No.1. That there are plenty of Scriptures validating a truth. No. 2. A person must look at the possibilities of the Greek or Hebrew word to see if there are words within the word that agrees with the many other clear valid verses. For instance, there are Hebrew and Greek words that can be rendered in reference to a man or woman; and it is the exact same word in the Hebrew or Greek. So a person needs to look at the verse that it is within the fuller meaning of the Greek or Hebrew word, as well as, many other valid verses to determine the accurate translation.

Let me give you an illustration: In I Timothy 2:15, the Bible says, *"**Notwithstanding she shall be saved** in child-bearing, if they continue in faith...."* (Note: The italicized phrase is the single Greek word, "sozo". Sozo's fuller meaning is: safety, save, deliver or protect, heal, preserve, do well, make whole). There are no words within this Greek word that could possibly be in reference to man or woman. However, according to the chapter, verse and the full meaning of the Bible, it can accurately be translated in reference to a man or a woman.

In I Timothy 2:15, it is clear for this word to be translated in reference to a woman.

Matthew 6:24 is another good example: "No **man** can serve two masters:" (The word, "man" is the Greek word, "oudeis" and is translated accurately as: man, woman or thing. "Oudeis" is used in the New Testament 230 times.

Another good example is the Greek word, "pais" This Greek word is translated as, "maid" in Luke 8:54: "And He put them all out, and took her by the hand, and called, saying, **_maid_**, arise."

The same Greek word, "pais" is translated as: **menservants** in Luke 12:45; "But and if that servant say in his heart, My lord delayeth His coming; and shall begin to beat the **menservants** and maidens ...."

Let's study on with Romans 1:18-20. Notice in verse 18, unrighteous people holding God's truth in unrighteousness. Keep in mind, the word "truth" throughout the Scriptures is in reference to God's Word (John 17:17 ...thy Word is truth). So they are keeping not all of God's Word, but some of it while they are unrighteousness. Look at verse 19: "... that which is known of God is manifest in them; for God hath showed it unto them. V.19. Lets us know what these unrighteous people are holding, experiencing in their lives. It's something that God has showed to them. V.20, *For the invisible* things of Him from the creation of the world are clearly *seen*...." (Note: The italicized phrase, "For the invisible" is the Greek word, "aoratos"). The definition of this word says it is compared to the Greek word, "Optanomai's" which has the fuller meaning as: *to discern clearly, mentally, experience, with wide open eyes, as at something remarkable; appear, look, see, shew self, to discern clearly (physically or mentally); to experience; to appear:—behold, perceive, see, take heed.*

Also notice the italicized word, "seen" in verse 20 is the Greek word, "kathorao". "Kathorao" is taken from the Greek word, "optanomai".

Very obviously, it is clear that God was telling us that ungodly, unrighteous people were holding the truths of God about imagination.

Again, they could only be doing this with the measure of faith that God gives to all of humanity, and I am extremely sure they were not using God's Ordained Imagination. How much more will it work for the righteous! II Corinthians 5:21: " He who knew no sin - became sin for us - that we would be the righteousness of God in Christ Jesus."

How much more is God's Ordained Imagination to work for us that are born again, Spirit-filled Christians. If it will work for a sinner, how much more will it work for you!

Understanding Simple but
God Ordained Imagination

God ordained the whole human race to have and to use their imagination. Every little child before they can ever read or write uses God's ordained imagination to be blessed. Once knowledge has been introduced to them they can imagine. For instance, you can give a little child the first time an apple. And from that time on they can see with their mind's eye an apple. If they ask for an apple that is not in the seen world, and you try to give them a banana, they know the difference. They can see into the invisible world with their mind's eye, with their imagination. The mind's eye, the imagination is activated by knowledge. An apple is natural knowledge placed into a person's mind; HOW MUCH MORE WILL SUPERNATURAL KNOWLEDGE PLACED IN OUR MIND ACTIVATE OUR IMAGINATION! God's Word is supernatural knowledge. And God's Word says, "Let this mind be in you, which was in Christ" — Philippians 2:5.

If Jesus were standing in the presence of someone, He could, any time He wanted to, "Look into their body and see if there was a dark image which would be a demon spirit."

So can you!

God has Ordained us to use our imagination to bring the blessings, the Supernatural of God from the Spirit world, from the Word of God into our natural life!

Humorous, but true.

In the Old Testament in the book of Numbers 22:23-31, you read the story where Balaam was riding his donkey and the donkey saw an angel, and Balaam and his two servants did not see the angel. The Scriptures go on to say that Balaam smote his donkey with his staff and then the Lord opened up the mouth of the donkey and the donkey spoke to

Balaam twice. Notice, as you read this passage, that *the donkey saw into the Spirit world*. The donkey saw an angel, and Balaam and his two servants did not see the angel. Secondly, the donkey spoke twice.

My point is this: If God can use a donkey that is incapable of being born again; God can use any human being. The donkey saw into the Spirit world, how much more can you see into the Spirit world.

Resources by Mel Bond

Releasing God's Anointing

God's Last Day's People

Neglecting Signs and Wonders Is Neglecting The Rapture

Understanding Your Worst Enemy

Heaven Declares Christians' Greatest Problem

Unimaginable Love

Mystery Of The Ages

Why Jesus Appears To People Today

Come Up Higher (Donna Bond's Music CD)

P 54